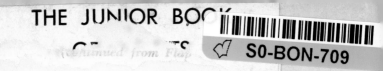

THE JUNIOR BOOK
OF INSECTS

E·P·DUTTON & CO. INC
1852   1954
CREATIVE·102 YEARS·PUBLISHING

By EDWIN WAY TEALE

THE JUNIOR BOOK OF
INSECTS

Interesting Facts about the Lives and Habits of the Common Insects together with Simple Instructions for Collecting, Rearing, and Studying Them.

By

EDWIN WAY TEALE

Illustrated with Photographs and Drawings by the Author

E. P. DUTTON & COMPANY, INC. • NEW YORK

Library of Congress Catalog Card Number: 52-12966

AMERICAN BOOK—STRATFORD PRESS, INC., NEW YORK

DEDICATED TO

DAVID

MY SON, THE

FIRST BOY TO READ THESE PAGES

A Note to You

WHEN I put down the first words of Chapter One, winter winds were rushing through the bare branches outside my window. Now, as I write these final words and the book is finished, autumn is well advanced. Another winter is almost here. In the meantime, the vast hordes of the insects, the million and one six-legged creatures, have come and gone.

Oftentimes, boys have the feeling that there is little left in the world for them to do; that everything worth while has been done. If you ever feel that way, remember these unnumbered insects about which we know so little. A famous entomologist once said to me: "I would be willing to bet that I could take almost any insect and, by studying it, discover something nobody knew before. We have yet to learn the complete life cycle of ninety-eight per cent of the insects. Even among the commonest six-legged creatures of the backyard, we know the life story of hardly more than one in twenty."

This vast realm is left for the boys of today to explore. In this world of little creatures, there are a legion mysteries to be solved. In writing this book, I have tried to give you a glimpse of the fascinating things you will find if you start backyard explorations of your own.

7

For assistance of various kinds during the preparing of this volume, I owe a debt of thanks to a number of friends. Especially am I indebted to Dr. Frank E. Lutz, of the American Museum of Natural History, for reading the book in manuscript form and making invaluable suggestions.

POSTSCRIPT

More than a dozen autumns have come and gone since I wrote the above Note to You. Now, for a seventh and revised edition, I add this postscript. First let me thank the many readers who have become my friends through their letters of encouragement and help. When I began revising these pages, I found there was little to change but a number of things to add. The ways of the insects alter little; it is our knowledge of them that continues to expand. It is my hope that you who read this book will help make that knowledge grow.

January 1953.   EDWIN WAY TEALE

Contents

10   Contents

List of Photographs

List of Drawings

THE JUNIOR BOOK
OF INSECTS

Chapter I

THE INSECT WORLD

YEARS ago, on my grandfather's farm in northern
Indiana, a sandy ridge rose above the surrounding
marshland, half a mile below the farmhouse. We used
to call the ridge "the island." Legend had it that long
ago it had been the scene of an Indian battle. On hot
summer days, I would spend hours there, wiggling
my bare toes in the warm sand, hunting for arrowheads. When I was ten or so, I had collected more
than 100 spearheads, arrowheads and tomahawk heads
from the sandy soil.

Evenings, my grandfather used to tell stories of the
pioneer days when he had seen as many as twenty deer
feeding at dawn in the lower meadow. By my time,
however, all the Indians and all the deer were gone.
The last lynx seen in that region was killed the very
year I was born. Pioneer days, with their wildcats and
wolves, Indians and deer, had passed over the horizon.

But, on that sand-dune farm, I found hunting adventures just the same. Instead of wildcats and wolves,
I stalked small and curious creatures of the insect
world. I spent hours watching ants laboring among the
chips of the woodyard. I followed the work of the

mud-dauber wasps building their nests in the granary. I poked woolly-bear caterpillars to make them curl up into red and black "pincushions."

At night, great moths used to come from the neighboring swamp and flutter against the lamp-lighted window screens. All these creatures were strange and fascinating to my young eyes. How strange they really were I did not learn until later on. For, the more we study and learn about the lives and habits of the insects, the more interesting and mysterious they become.

I still remember the exciting moment when I first discovered half a dozen black ants busily "milking their cows"—stroking the backs of green plant lice with their feelers to make them give drops of honeydew. I remember the excitement of my first glimpse of a grasshopper changing its skin. I was told it was also changing its skeleton,—for an insect wears its skeleton on the outside instead of on the inside of its body. I remember the day I first saw a carrot worm, green and black and yellow, lean back on a loop of silk, begin to shiver, and then gradually turn into a greenish-gray chrysalis out of which, later on, came the resplendent black swallowtail butterfly.

All around us, as soon as we come to know something of the wonderful life of the insects, we find absorbing things taking place. There are so many insects and so few people who pay much attention to them that there are many things yet to learn about their ways and abilities. Today, your chances would be slight, even in the jungles of Africa or on the upper reaches of the Amazon, of finding a new kind of four-legged animal unknown to science. But among the host of six-legged insects, new discoveries are being made, all the time. Boys, as well as men, have added to our knowledge of the insect world.

On a farm in Switzerland, many years ago, a small boy lay watching a battle of the ants. A horde of red invaders had marched into the farmyard from the edge of a neighboring wood and had fallen upon the smaller ants of the garden colony. At the end of an hour, the battlefield was strewn with dead and the robber insects were carrying away the children of their victims.

The boy followed them. He found little ants like those in his own garden serving as slaves in the nest of the invaders,—feeding and caring for their masters. At the age of ten, this boy made a discovery which had escaped all the great scientists before him. Throughout the rest of his life, he continued to study the insects. He became known all over the world as Auguste Forel, the great authority on ants.

A few years ago, another boy stayed awake twenty-four hours to solve a mystery of natural history right in his own backyard. For decades, scientists in Brazil had been baffled by the manner in which insects fell prey to a common garden spider of the region. Nobody had ever seen it make a web. The boy determined to watch the spider day and night until he saw it catch an insect. Just before dawn, he observed it hurriedly spin a little net of silk and catch half a dozen leaf hoppers, tiny insects that flew only in the hours before sunrise. Then, before it was entirely light, the spider unfastened its web, folded it carefully, "threw it over its shoulder like a sack of potatoes," and retired to dine on the contents at leisure.

A third boy, living in the south of France, spent the first month's salary he ever earned for an illustrated book on insects. Years later, he wrote: "As I turned the pages for the hundredth time, a voice whispered vaguely: 'Thou, too, shalt become an historian of animals!' " The boy's name was Jean Henri Fabre. He grew up to become famous as "The Homer of the Insects." Until he was more than eighty years old, Fabre continued to observe and study the ways of these small creatures. He made hundreds of discoveries and recorded his fascinating adventures in a long series of books which have been translated into most of the languages of the world. One of the best of his volumes for you to begin with is called *Insect Adventures*.

The thing to remember is that no matter where you live—East, West, North or South—you, too, can have insect adventures of your own. Without any expensive equipment and with spare hours as your only time, you can find exciting hunting close at home. If you want to observe some of the strangest creatures in the world, all you have to do is to step out in your own backyard! Here you find creatures that smell with fernlike feelers; creatures that hear with ears located on their legs; creatures that fly only once and bite off their wings when they land! Within sight of your own doorstep, you can find amazing six-legged animals that make paper, dig tunnels and produce silk! Within the boundaries of your own horizon, you can encounter small creatures that use pincers, drills, hammers and rakes!

When you enter the wonder-world of the insects, I have discovered, your adventures are limited largely by the extent of your knowledge. You make progress in exploring this world on two legs: interest and knowledge. If you are interested but don't know what to look for, you are like a one-legged man and hobble along getting only half the fun you might. Even the commonest cricket or katydid, if you learn enough of its life and habits, becomes intensely interesting. As a whole, the insects are interesting to us because they are so old, so strange, so numerous and so important.

I. They are so old.

Farmers along the shores of the Baltic Sea many years ago began picking up pieces of transparent amber which had been washed up by the waves. Millions of years before, this amber had been pitch oozing from the great prehistoric evergreen trees of northern Europe. Insects were caught in the sticky fluid which hardened with the passing of time. The amber formed transparent tombs for the insects, some of them ants and wasps almost exactly like those you see on any summer day. Thus we know that 30,000,000 years ago, long before man appeared on earth, the insects were here.

Before the first bird flew, insects were navigating the air on wings. Before the first ancestor of the bluebird or robin burst into song, crickets were fiddling away to produce their chirping solos. Before any warm-blooded animal of any kind roamed the earth, the insect tribes were well established.

The next time you watch an ant crawling along a sidewalk, a bee droning from flower to flower, or a beetle toiling up the stalk of a weed, remember that you are looking at tiny forms of life that have been familiar to the earth since prehistoric days. Because the insects appeared so early in the history of the world and have endured so long, we look at them with added interest.

II. They are so strange.

Can you imagine a mother with 10,000,000 children? Can you imagine walking backward all your life? Can you imagine living on a diet of mustard plasters and cayenne pepper? Can you imagine looking at the world through eyes having 60,000 lenses instead of two?

Yet, all those amazing things occur among the insects. Tropical termite queens lay as many as 10,-000,000 eggs in a lifetime; ant lions, or doodlebugs, always walk backward; certain small beetles consider a mustard plaster a great delicacy; and some dragonflies have 30,000 lenses in a single eye.

Oftentimes, when I used to watch ants and bees and mud-dauber wasps as a boy, I used to wonder how they found their way home after wandering far afield. Follow a bumblebee sometime and you will find it buzzes from flower to flower in an aimless fashion, flying from field to field until it is laden with nectar and pollen. Then it makes a "beeline" for home. What tells it the direction to fly? In the autumn, you see Monarch butterflies gathering into great straggling flocks for the long migration to warm Southern states. None of these insects have ever made that flight before. Yet, traveling sometimes with the wind and sometimes against it, they journey hundreds and even thousands of miles—from as far as Hudson Bay to the Gulf states. How do they find their way?

The mysteries we find in the world of the insects often puzzle us. But, at the same time, they increase our interest in the six-legged creatures we are watching.

III. They are so numerous.

Tonight, before you go to bed, if the sky is clear, go out and look up at the stars. The whole heavens seem filled with them. Yet if you counted each star you can see with the naked eye, the number would be only about one-one-hundredth the number of different kinds of insects already known to science.

Some years, as many as 6,000 new species are added to the lists. All told, approximately 625,000 kinds of six-legged creatures have been described and named.

This total is greater than the total number of plants, animals and birds put together. Yet, there is a vast army of insects yet to be classified. Some authorities believe there are as many as 10,000,000 kinds of insects in the world.

And each kind is represented by an infinite number of individuals. If you counted all the chinch bugs in a single acre of infested wheat, I have been told, you would find as many as 60,000,000 insects! A dragonfly may drop nearly 100,000 eggs into the water at one time. If enemies of the insects did not consume vast numbers, we would soon be eaten out of house and home. But the fact that there are so many kinds of insects and so many of each kind insures that we will have good hunting and plenty of opportunities to watch interesting things going on around us.

One surprising thing you will soon discover. Unlike larger animals, the insects appear in several forms during their lifetime. The immature creature oftentimes bears little resemblance to the adult. Thus, a "baby" moth is a crawling caterpillar and a "baby" dragonfly an underwater nymph living the life of a fish. However, every true insect has two things in common when it becomes an adult: a jointed body and no more than six jointed legs. Spiders and daddy longlegs, with eight instead of six legs, are not true insects. Instead they are relatives of the crabs and scorpions.

When you receive a letter, it always has four things in the address: your name, your street address, the town and the state in which you live. Similarly, in dividing up the vast numbers of insects, scientists give them a sort of address which enables us to locate them exactly. The largest divisions are the *orders*. These in turn are divided into smaller divisions called *families*. The families are subdivided into groups each known as a *genus*. And, finally, there are the *species*, or different kinds of insects within each genus. Some of the main orders of insects are *Lepidoptera*, the butterflies and moths; *Coleoptera*, the beetles; *Diptera*, the flies; *Odonata*, the dragonflies; *Orthoptera*, the crickets and grasshoppers; and *Hymenoptera*, the bees, ants and wasps.

IV. They are so important.

You and I, and all the rest of mankind, it has been estimated, could live on this earth only nine years if all the birds should disappear. The insects, without the birds to keep them in check, would multiply rapidly and devour every green thing growing in the ground. A single bird sometimes kills as many as 1,000 insects a day. In the State of Massachusetts, alone, one scientist has calculated, birds consume 21,000 bushels of insects every twenty-four hours during the summer months. And, it takes about 120,000 average-sized insects to fill a bushel basket!

Farmers spend $100,000,000 a year fighting insect pests. Yet, these hungry hordes devour one-tenth of everything that grows on American farms. The annual loss is put at $3,000,000,000. Armies of men are fighting the boll weevil, the gypsy moth, the corn borer and the Japanese beetle. The harm that insects do, makes them important.

But the good they do also makes them important. Hardly one per cent of the insects do any harm to man. And many of the other ninety-nine per cent do good. Without the tongue of the bumblebee, for example, the valuable crop of red clover might be unknown; without the honeybee, orchards and gardens would be less productive. Both insects carry pollen from flower to flower and so fertilize the blooms.

Just try, sometime, imagining what sort of a world this would be if there were no insects in it. There would be few flowers because there would be no insects to pollenize them. There would be no silk, no shellac, no honey because all three are the product of six-legged workers. There would be few if any song birds because without the living food of insects and the seeds produced by insect-fertilized plants, most birds would starve. So, a world without insects would be a drab and colorless place,—a world without honey, without birds, without flowers and without fruits.

Besides the four interests which living insects hold for us—the fact they are so old, so strange, so numerous and so important—these six-legged creatures have an additional attraction: the fun they provide for the collector. Hunting butterflies and beetles, moths and dragonflies, provides us with a hobby that keeps us outdoors in summer and engaged in absorbing work during spare time in winter. The fun of this sport will be dealt with in the next chapter.

One beauty of it is that you can start anywhere. Dr. Frank E. Lutz, of the American Museum of Natural History, in New York City, found more than 1,000 different kinds of insects in one backyard. So, whether you live in the country, in a village or in a big city, insect hunting is within your reach. And the sport of watching and collecting these small but fascinating creatures is one which will last through the years.

Chapter II

THE FUN OF COLLECTING INSECTS

COLLECTING insects is like reaching into a grab-bag. You never know what you are going to pull from your net. There are so many thousands of six-legged creatures around us that you are always finding something new, something you have never seen before. The unexpected adds to your fun.

One amateur insect hunter, a few years ago, was driving on a winding mountain road in California. Ahead, he saw several brilliant black and yellow butterflies circling and alighting at a moist spot on the road. Creeping forward little by little, he scooped up one of the bright-winged creatures in his net. At home, he was unable to identify it in any of his reference books. When he sent it to a famous authority, he discovered that it was a new species of swallowtail, a butterfly unlike any other on record. Scientists have given it the name of Rudkin's Swallowtail in honor of the discoverer.

Charles Darwin, one of the greatest natural scientists, recalled, when he was a very old man, the thrill he got as a boy when he found a new kind of beetle and saw it displayed with a card bearing the words: "Captured by C. Darwin, Esq."

If you are persistent and lucky, there is always the chance, even if it is remote, that you will pull from your net an insect that is not only new to you but new to science as well. Even if you never do this, you will still have abundant fun and profit from your hobby. It is one which will take you afield in the fresh air and the sunshine. It aids your health while it interests your mind. And, it gives you plenty of exercise, as you will find when you finish your first exploration-trips into the insect world. In fact, one star football player on a Western team made it a practice to keep in condition during the summer by chasing butter-flies!

Many boys who have begun collecting insects as a youthful hobby have kept it up the rest of their lives. The longer you collect the more fun it becomes.

Many years ago, a boy in Pennsylvania began making a collection of butterflies. He started with the Monarchs and swallowtails and cabbage butterflies, just the kinds you will find in any backyard. As the years passed, his collection grew. When he died it was so valuable it was purchased by the Field Museum of Natural History, in Chicago, for $20,000. This collector, who started as a boy, was Dr. Herman Strecker.

Another famous collection, which was built up over a long period of years, belonged to Dr. William Barnes, of Decatur, Illinois. It contained more than 300,000 butterflies and moths which had been captured in all parts of the world. When the United States Government purchased the collection for its National Museum, in Washington, the vast assemblage of mounted insects made the journey East in a special express car. Like Dr. Strecker, Dr. Barnes began his collecting when he was a boy.

Insect-hunting is also a hobby that frequently leads to a career. Many of the famous entomologists of the country first became interested in the study of "bugs" through collecting in their youth. And, here is a tip for increasing the fun of the sport: Collect facts and observations as well as specimens. Living insects are more interesting than dead ones. Try to find out all you can about the lives and abilities of the tiny creatures you scoop up with your net. Then, the farther you go, the more fun you will have in your hobby of exploring the insects.

As time passes you will want to read other books about the six-legged creatures you meet. At the end of this volume, you will find listed a number of books containing additional information about the different insects. Now, for outfitting your expedition into the weed jungles where the insects live. You will need a net and a few other simple aids. Most of this equipment you can make yourself. How to do it will be told in the next chapter.

Chapter III

MAKING YOUR EQUIPMENT

WITHOUT any other equipment than a pair of sharp eyes, you can begin having fun watching the insects. But, if you take up the sport of collecting, you will require several aids. With the following list of items, you will be well equipped for home exploring and for bringing back the interesting creatures you meet.

A Butterfly Net
A Killing Bottle
A Pair of Tweezers
A Strong Jackknife
A Collection of Jars, Tins and Pillboxes
A Notebook
A Magnifying Glass
The Fieldbook of Insects by Dr. Frank E. Lutz

The most expensive items on the list are the last two. A combined magnifying glass and ruler, such as you can buy at a nickel-and-dime store, will be satisfactory at first for getting a better view of the insects. But, when you get to the really tiny folk of the backyard jungles, a good enlarging glass will be needed.

Similarly, you can get along without the *Fieldbook*

for a time. You can start with the butterflies and use
a ten-cent-store butterfly guide. But, sooner or later,
if you want to learn the names and characteristics of
the creatures you meet, Lutz's book will become indis-
pensable. It is the classic "road map" for tourists in
Insect Land.

For less than a dollar, you can purchase a butterfly
net already made. But, for a few cents, you can make
one yourself. In either case, you will find that a good
net is one of the most important items on your list.
A few insects will hold still long enough for you to
watch them, but the vast majority are lively fellows
which "stay put" only when they have to.

There are a number of ways of constructing a serv-
iceable net. I will start with the simplest. The materials required are:

> An old broomhandle
> A piece of heavy wire, about 32 inches long
> A strip of mosquito netting, 3 feet by 2½ feet
> A roll of tire tape

Begin by sawing off the broomhandle so it is about
three feet long. Then, on opposite sides of the sawed-
off end, chisel out grooves that are approximately four
inches long and a little wider than the diameter of
your wire. After you have bent the wire into a circle with a four-inch "leg" at each end, fit the parallel
legs into the grooves and wrap tire tape around and
around, binding the wire to the broomhandle as is
shown in Fig. 1.

open space in the tube. When the net is not in use, the handle can be removed and the whole stored in a small space.

Another way of achieving the same end is to obtain a discarded fishing rod. Use the butt end as the handle with the ferrule of the next section employed as the tube holding the head of the net. In some cases, special nets have been constructed with jointed handles which could be made longer or shorter by adding or taking away sections.

An entirely different kind of a net will provide great sport after you have become acquainted with the larger and more common insects and are seeking new and tinier creatures to watch and identify. This is what is known as a sweeping net. With it, you walk through grass and weeds sweeping the net back and forth, collecting curious forms of life. Looking into your net almost always brings a surprise or two. You can sweep at night as well as during the day, getting different kinds of insects in dark and in daylight.

Because of the punishment such a net receives, it has to be made extra strong. An ordinary outfit will soon wear out if it is used for sweeping. So, make the bag of the sweep net of light duck or strong muslin. Sometimes, the handle is extended clear across the ring as shown in Fig. 5. This gives extra support to the bag and eases the strain on the wire ring supporting the cloth. It is usually a good idea, if going any distance from home on an insect-hunting expedition, to take

Everything is now complete except making and attaching the bag of the net. Fold your piece of mosquito netting and cut it into the shape indicated in Fig. 2. The top of this blunt-nosed cone should have the same

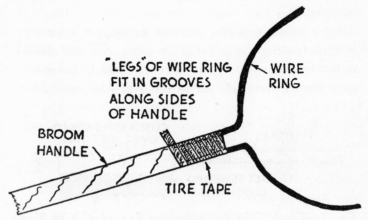

Fig. 1.—How to Attach Net Ring to Handle.

circumference as the wire hoop. But it should not be sewed directly to the wire. Instead, a narrow strip of light muslin or canvas should be sewed over the wire

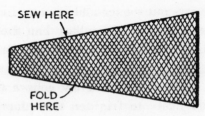

Fig. 2.—Shape to Cut Bag of Net.

and the netting attached to this, as shown in Fig. 3. If this procedure is followed, there is less likelihood of the netting pulling away from the ring.

The bag should always be between one and a half and two times as long as the diameter of the ring. This enables you to give the net a twist, when you have captured an insect, folding the bag over the wire and preventing the prisoner's escape. The bag should never be cut with square corners. Insects lodged in such corners are difficult to remove. Also, never cut

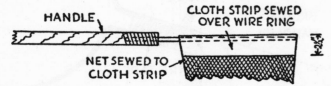

Fig. 3.—Cloth Strip for Attaching Bag of Net to Ring.

the bag with a narrow peak. The small end should be rounded and never narrower than four inches. Large butterflies and moths, if caught in narrow quarters, almost invariably damage their wings.

While mosquito netting is the cheapest material you can use, it wears out sooner and is more likely to become torn on bushes and brambles than the more expensive kinds of netting such as bobbinet, Brussels and silk bolting cloth. Some insect hunters always dye their nets brown, black or green. They believe that white nets are more likely to frighten the quarry as they approach.

If you want to make a demountable net, in which the bag and hoop can be taken off from the handle, you follow the procedure shown in Fig. 4. Get a metal tube about six inches long and three-quarters of an inch in diameter. Push one end into a container of perfectly dry sand until the sand is slightly more than

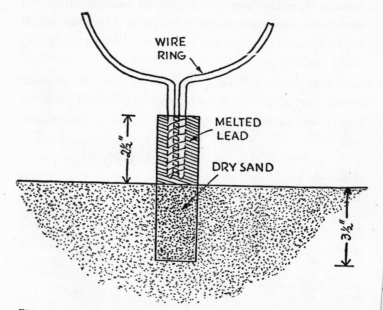

Fig. 4.—Method of Making a Demountable Butterfly Net.

halfway up the tube. Then, after binding the two "legs" of the ring together, insert them in the open end and pour in melted lead until the tube is full. After the metal has cooled, the sand can be poured out of the other end and the handle inserted in the

along a needle and thread. A torn net, in fields filled with insects, will ruin the day if you have no means of repairing the damage.

After you have caught your insects, you need a killing bottle to put them to sleep as quickly and painlessly as possible. Regular collectors use a cyanide jar. However, the chemical is deadly poison and care must

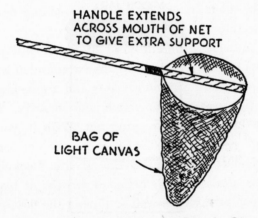

HANDLE EXTENDS
ACROSS MOUTH OF NET
TO GIVE EXTRA SUPPORT

BAG OF
LIGHT CANVAS

Fig. 5.—How Handle Extends Across Ring to Give Added Strength in Sweeping Net.

be used in handling it. For ordinary purposes, carbon tetrachloride is satisfactory for use in a killing bottle. It can be purchased as Carbona, a cleaning compound, at any drugstore. Wet a wad of cotton batting with the fluid and place it in the bottom of a wide-mouthed container, such as a pint Mason jar. Over the wad, it is a good idea to place a piece of wire screen, cut to fit, as is shown in Fig. 6. This prevents the insects from getting wet or from crawling under the cotton batting.

What to do with your specimens after they have been killed will be taken up in a later chapter. For carrying them home and for holding live insects, you will find it useful to have a collection of empty bot-

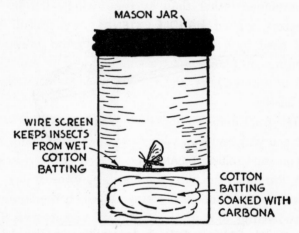

MASON JAR

WIRE SCREEN
KEEPS INSECTS
FROM WET
COTTON
BATTING

COTTON
BATTING
SOAKED WITH
CARBONA

Fig. 6.—An Insect-Killing Bottle.

tles, tins and jars. You can save these as you find them and store them away for a time of need.

For collecting small, delicate, soft-bodied insects, such as plant lice, supply houses sell what is known as an aspirator. It consists of a glass bottle with a rubber stopper and two rubber tubes. The collector draws air in through one tube and the insects at the end of the other tube are drawn into the bottle. A screen prevents them from being sucked into the other tube. If you develop a special interest in minute insects, you can make such a device for use in collecting the fragile creatures.

In handling most insects, and especially butterflies and moths, always use tweezers instead of your fingers. If this is impossible, pick them up by their legs or antennae rather than by their wings. Besides the tweezers, a good jackknife will be found useful. You will need it to cut off twigs, to examine galls—the swellings on plants and trees made by some insects,—and to remove bark and rotting wood in your search for beetles.

The final item—a notebook—may sound like work. But you will find that your fun is increased many fold if you start taking down notes on the insects you collect. Put down the date, the place, the time of day, the weather conditions, the plants on which the creatures were feeding, and anything unusual you observe. Such notes will teach you where to look for certain insects, at what seasons the different species are most plentiful, how weather conditions affect their habits and what plants or flowers they prefer. It will add information which will make your collection really worth while.

If you trust to your memory, you are bound to make mistakes. So, get into the habit of jotting down your notes at the time you make a catch. Hence, the value of a sturdy notebook and a couple of pencil stubs which will fit in your pocket without danger of breaking.

Now, with our net, killing bottle, notebook and a few odd jars and tins, we are ready to start invading the insect world. Probably the easiest game to hunt in the beginning will be the innumerable aunts and uncles, brothers and cousins of the beetle tribe.

Chapter IV

THE BEETLES

THE beetles are the Smiths of the insect world. Theirs is the largest tribe of all. If you collected all the kinds of beetles you can find on the North American continent alone, you would have 22,000 different insects. If you possessed one of each species of beetle known, your collection would be swelled to more than 150,000 specimens.

Some of them would be drab gray or dull black; others would be living jewels with scintillating metallic reds and blues. Some would come from rotting wood and under old stones; some would come from flowers; some even would come from tidal beaches where the water covered them part of the time. They would range from moving specks so small they could crawl through the eye of a needle to a tropical giant larger than a mouse.

But all these varied insects would have one thing in common, the distinguishing mark of the beetle. They would have characteristic shells on their backs. The fore wings have been changed into hard covers which protect the membranous hind wings with which the insects fly. Watch a ladybug alight on a leaf sometime and you will notice that as she settles down, her gauzy black hind wings fold themselves neatly and are tucked beneath the hard, shiny sheaths or cases formed by the fore wings. The beetles get the name of their order: Coleoptera (ko′-le-op′-tera), from this characteristic. The word comes from the Greek and means sheath-winged. During flight, the sheath-wings are held rigid while the filmy hind wings propel the beetle through the air.

You won't go very far with your insect exploring before you encounter members of the sheath-winged clan. Unless you are careful, you will find them right in the cases where you keep your collected specimens. Tiny Dermestids, like carpet beetles, get among the mounted insects and feed upon them. If you begin to see fine brown dust beneath any of your specimens, you will know that these beetle pests are working within. How to get rid of them will be explained later on. Incidentally, some members of the beetle tribe have the camel beaten a dozen ways when it comes to doing without water. They have been known to live for long periods sealed in a bottle where there was nothing to drink!

Certain other beetles can't do without water at all. They live right in it in some cases and on the surface in others. The "whirligig bugs" you see spinning on the surface of a pond, for example, are beetles. Some carnivorous water beetles grow to an inch or more in length. They dive beneath the surface after their prey and remain submerged for long periods. Bubbles carried down in a thick coating of hairs, supply them with oxygen. While under water, they will attack tadpoles and even small fish.

One of the fiercest insects known is the Tiger Beetle. Its larvae make burrows in the sand along the beach or in hard-packed paths. Crouching just below the surface they wait to pounce on any insect that wanders near. Their burrows are sometimes called "disappearing holes." If you walk over the spot, a number of holes will appear in the ground. If you look back, after you have passed by, all the holes will have disappeared. The creatures, crouching within, descend into their burrows as you approach and come to the top, filling the opening of the holes with their heads, when you pass by.

The way to catch them is to sit down near a hole and remain perfectly quiet. Soon, the dirt-colored head will appear in the opening and if you are quick, you can scoop up the sand at the spot and bring the fierce beetle larva out where you can examine it closely. An interesting thing to note is the bulge or hump on the fifth segment of the abdomen. This hump is equipped with two hooks curving forward so they catch in the sides of the vertical burrow and help keep the insect from being jerked out of its hole when its jaws have clamped on the leg of the prey and it is struggling to drag its victim down into its lair.

The adult beetles, which are just as fierce as their larvae, stand erect on long and slender legs. If you chase them, they will fly swiftly for a few feet, alight,

turn and watch you approach, fly a few feet on again
and repeat the performance. Like a cottontail, they
often circle back to the same spot where you first saw
them, if you keep up the pursuit. Some tiger beetles
are metallic-blue, green or copper, with small buff
markings. Others living on the light sand of the sea-
shore may be white or pale yellow. This makes them
difficult to see until they move.

All beetles bite instead of sucking. Some that live in
the tropics have huge mandibles, or jaws, longer than
their bodies and lined with sharp teeth. The stag beetles of Europe are famous for their battles. The males
use their heavy jaws to battle like stag deer for the
favor of the females. If you have ever encountered
one of the American stag beetles, or pinching bugs,
around an electric light, you will understand the biting ability of these armored insects.

Other members of the beetle tribe use their sharp
jaws to nip out bits of food that range from fruit and
vegetables to cigarettes and red pepper! How valuable
or harmful a beetle is depends upon *what* it uses its
jaws to bite. Potato bugs cause millions of dollars in
damage every year by devouring the tender potato
plants. A relative, the ladybird beetle, on the other
hand, is so valuable that farmers buy millions of them
a year from dealers and let them loose in their orchards
and fields. Ladybugs use their jaws to eat plant lice
and scale insects.

Another beetle that helps us is the burying, or sex-
ton beetle. If a dead mouse is left in a backyard, even

in the heart of a city, these beetles will come from afar to feed upon it. Some species excavate under the body and bury it before they lay their eggs upon it. In France, Fabre played tricks on these busy little beetles by tying the mouse to weeds so it could not be buried. How the insects toiled hour after hour and finally succeeded in severing the bonds and completing their task is told in his volume, *The Wonders of Instinct*.

By removing carrion, such beetles make this a cleaner and more sanitary world. The dung beetles, or tumblebugs, which you meet rolling their balls of dung over the ground in a pasture or barnyard, are also members of the insect sanitary corps. The sacred scarab of the Nile, which was revered by the Egyptians thousands of years ago, was a brilliant metallic-winged insect of this type. The beetle was thought to symbolize the sun and its ball of dung the earth. Most carrion beetles you will meet will be broad, oval and rather flat. The common shades are black and brown with yellow or orange splotches. Being flat helps them crawl under the animals on which they feed.

While we are dealing with ill-smelling things, it is a good time to mention the strange Bombardier beetle. It has been using a gas attack for centuries to escape from its enemies! This little ground beetle, with a yellowish head and bluish body, lives under boards and flat stones and is usually found where it is damp. When attacked, it ejects from a gland at the tip of the abdomen a drop of fluid which turns into a jet of smoke-like gas when it comes in contact with the air.

This vapor halts the attacker, thus giving time for the beetle to scurry to safety. It can fire four or five "rounds" before its liquid ammunition is exhausted.

Blister, or oil, beetles have a different method of defense. They exude caustic oil from various joints. This yellowish fluid burns like acid when it touches the skin. In olden times the bodies of these beetles used to be ground up and made into blister plasters for use in treating ailments.

The life story of one of these oil beetles is as strange as a fairy tale. Out of the egg, which has been laid in the ground, hatches a tiny larva. It climbs to a flower where it waits patiently until a honeybee alights. Attaching itself firmly to the hairs on the bee's body, it soars away to the hive where it secretes itself in one of the cells stored with pollen or bee-bread. After the queen bee has laid an egg in the cell and closed it up, the larva devours both egg and food. Afterwards it molts and becomes a sluggish creature living on honey. It makes seven transformations before it attains the form of a full-fledged beetle.

For three years, the larva of the long-horned Capricorn beetle eats its way through the solid wood of an oak tree before it transforms into the adult. This grub has no eyes or ears. But it possesses a marvelous instinct that saves its life when it awakens from the deep sleep which bridges the gap between the three years of eating and the appearance of the armored, long-horned adult. Before this transformation sleep, the grub tun-

nels its way to the surface, then covers the entrance
with imitation wood formed of tiny bits cemented together. Finally, it always lies down facing out. If sleep
overtook the grub facing in, the heavily armored and
stiff adult would be unable to turn around in the burrow or to back out into the open air, and it would die
in its prison.

The curious and often beautiful galleries formed by
another wood-borer gives the insect the name of En-
graver beetle. Its activity takes place just under the
bark. The female, a little brown insect with its head
lengthened into a short snout or beak, channels out
the central gallery and at intervals along each side of
the tunnel digs little niches. In these she places her
eggs. Each egg develops into a larva which tunnels off
into the darkness away from the main gallery. In the
end, this series of branching tunnels, produced by the
work of a whole family, often resembles some fantastic centipede. Curiously enough, each species of En-
graver beetle has its characteristic pattern. You can
tell the species by the form of the pattern under the
bark. Some years ago, the U. S. Department of Agri-
culture estimated that these insects have destroyed a
billion dollars' worth of timber in the last fifty years.

Unlike the butterflies, beetles have very strong legs.
Those of the flea-beetles are developed so the insects
can spring away from a pursuer like tiny kangaroos.
Different species of these insects are found on grapes,
spinach and cucumbers.

Speaking of jumping—have you ever encountered one of the curious click beetles? If you haven't you have fun in store for you. These strange creatures jump with their "necks" instead of their legs!

Most of them are brown or black and develop from larvae which are known as "wire worms" and live in the ground, feeding on the roots of grasses. Ordinary beetles paw the air with their legs, like a turtle, when they are placed on their backs. But not the click beetles. They lie still for a moment, then snap their heads back so they are thrown upward into the air, often turning over in the process. If they alight on their feet, off they run. If they don't, they try again.

Sometimes, you will see long, rather drab, short-legged beetles crawling about on vegetation. They seem uninteresting in the daytime. But at night they become one of the most attractive of the insects. For they are the "fireflies." The ends of the abdomen of these beetles give off a greenish-yellow glow in the darkness. In some species the larvae and the eggs, as well as the adults, are luminous. The tropical fireflies are more brilliant than ours. Once, an American army surgeon completed an operation by the light of a glass jar filled with such insects. Travelers tell of seeing frogs in Central America that seemed to have fire glowing inside their bodies. They had devoured a number of luminous beetles.

Just how the light is produced is still a puzzle. It is known that the combination of oxygen with a mysterious substance called luciferin, produces the heatless illumination. In laboratories, scientists have tried to reproduce the effect artificially, but have failed. Underneath the light-producing surface on the body of the firefly is a reflecting surface, just as a locomotive headlight has a burnished reflector behind it.

In some species, the females are wingless and remain in the grass, where their flashing signals attract the males flying overhead. Such wingless females are known as glowworms. The average intensity of ten different specimens of fireflies tested at the Smithsonian Institution, in Washington, was found to be about 1-50,000 candle-power. The material which produces this light will keep for years. In one case, luciferin was kept in an airtight bottle for two years and when soaked in water, it gave off its characteristic glow. Because oxygen is needed to produce their flameless light, fireflies require more air than is the case with other insects. They will die in a closed container long before most other beetles.

In an order as big as the beetle's, all I can hope to do is to introduce you to some of the members; others you will meet for yourself. You will meet the big blundering Junebug—which is not a bug and often doesn't come in June but in May. You will meet the destructive little rose chafer, relative of the sacred Scarab. And perhaps you will meet some of the "queer cousins" of the clan. There are blind beetles found only beneath huge boulders sunk deep in the ground. There are pale ghostly beetles that live deep in limestone caves and never see the light. There are ant-

loving beetles which live in the nests of these insects
and sometimes ride around on the backs of their hosts.
And there are Drugstore beetles which dine on at least
forty-five different kinds of drugs, including the poi-
sons aconite and belladonna!

Chapter V

BEETLE HUNTING

ONE autumn morning, in the sand-dune country of northern Indiana, I tramped for nearly a mile along the shore of Lake Michigan following a thin, wavering line of dead beetles. The insects had flown out over the lake, had been drowned, and their bodies had been washed high on the sand by the waves.

Oftentimes, you can make a rich harvest of such insects along the shores of a large body of water. By "beachcombing" for beetles in this way, you can add as many as fifty or a hundred new species to your collection in the course of a single day. So, if you live near the Great Lakes or the sea, let the waves work for you.

Along creeks and streams, after floods or spring freshets, you find another source of beetle specimens. Look in the masses of debris which collect among bushes and lodge against tree trunks. A good way to sort over such masses of sticks and straws is to spread the material out on the sand or on newspapers or a piece of white oilcloth. In this way, you can "winnow" out beetles which have collected in the rubbish.

Sometimes, you can drive out the insects by dropping a little ammonia on the top of a pile of rubbish. The fumes drive out the beetles and you can catch them as they appear.

In early spring, when the beetles are still drowsy, you can use a sieve as an aid to collecting them. Gather masses of dead leaves and moldering trash under the trees of a wood and put the debris in the sieve. Shaking it, causes the finer material, including the small beetles to fall out while the sticks and leaves remain in the sieve.

There are, in fact, more ways of hunting beetles than there are of capturing almost any other kind of insect. Another method of collecting consists of going along like an old bear, turning over flat rocks. Under such stones, especially where the ground is moist, you will find a wide variety of beetles. Where the soil is dry, only during the rainy seasons—in spring and autumn—will you have much success in hunting under stones. But in woods and where there is shade and in lowland meadows, keep your eyes open for flat stones partially sunk in the ground.

Always make it a rule to put back every stone just where you found it. In certain sections of the country a few species of beetles have become almost unknown because collectors failed to follow this rule. They not only took away some of the beetles but left the natural homes of the others destroyed by their carelessness. When you go insect hunting, leave things as you find them. You may want to pass that way again.

Of course, rotten stumps and old logs are happy

hunting grounds for beetles. The best logs are those in shady places and moist surroundings. Logs exposed to the scorching sun less often contribute to your collection. "Red rotten" logs are usually better than "white rotten" ones. For two or three years after a large tree dies, it is the home of many beetles. After the wood is thoroughly dry, however, the coleoptera population decreases. So examine under the bark of dead and dying trees. In this way you can uncover many interesting additions to your collection.

A trick you can use sometimes to attract various wood beetles is to cut a number of branches and tie them to the trunk of a tree or place them in a compact bundle on the ground in the shade. When the branches begin to dry out, they attract the beetles. All you have to do is make the rounds of your bundles, shaking them over a cloth or newspaper. It is best to put branches of the same kind together in one bundle.

Another bit of strategy you can use in beetle hunting is to bury tin cans and olive jars in the ground. Have the tops just flush with the ground and place a bit of meat, boiled egg or fried fish in the bottom of the container as shown in Fig. 7. This bait attracts the beetles which tumble into the bottle or can and are unable to climb up the sides again. When you make the rounds of your "trap line" in the morning, you may find half a dozen or more beetles in a single olive jar.

Without the use of traps, you can attract carrion beetles by putting a dead mouse or fish in some isolated

spot. Coming from all around, the beetles will be discovered under the decaying flesh. While this is not a
pleasant form of hunting, it supplies some beautiful
additions to your varied assemblage of sheath-winged
insects.

Some collectors make use of an old umbrella to
gather beetles which live on the foliage of bushes and

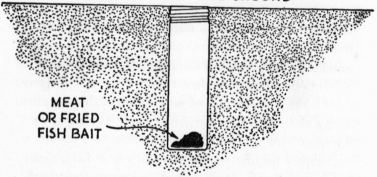

OLIVE BOTTLE BURIED WITH OPEN
TOP FLUSH WITH THE GROUND

MEAT
OR FRIED
FISH BAIT

Fig. 7.—Beetle Trap.

small trees. They hold the umbrella upside down under a tree or bush and then tap the branches above it
smartly with a stick. The beetles let go their hold and
drop into the umbrella.

A few of the most active beetles, such as the ferocious tigers, must be caught in a net. Others that spend
their lives in the weed and grass tangles of lowland
fields can be caught by sweeping. For the tiniest of the

beetles, you can use a pillbox if you practice handling it beforehand.

Take the pillbox in your hand and place the first finger above the box and the little finger below it, having the thumb on one side of the box and the two middle fingers on the other side. After you have practiced it several times, you will be able to work the two halves of the box like jaws, snapping up little beetles from leaves and other resting places.

Certain flowers which bloom in the fall, such as goldenrod, attract many beetles. Also, chestnut trees in bloom always bring a large number of beetles to them.

Along the sandy shores of lakes and the sea, interesting little beetles can often be discovered by pulling up bunches of isolated grass and examining among the roots. Moss on the banks of sheltered streams should be examined for beetles. Shake the moss over sand or a paper to dislodge the insects within it. In winter, many of the smaller species hibernate under moss and bark.

After spring floods have covered low pasturelands, keep your eyes open for drowned dung beetles, or tumblebugs. The receding waters often leave these large insects behind. Besides drowning them out, the flood waters clean them perfectly.

As a general rule, the best hunting places for beetles are in isolated trees, along hedges and at the edge of a wood. In deep woodland spots, there are fewer beetles than at the edges of the woods.

When autumn comes, keep your eye on toadstools.

Many beetles dine on toadstools and other forms of fungus. They seem to prefer those which are partially decomposed. Puffballs also attract them. In gathering specimens here, examine in the ground around the spot as well as on the puffball or toadstool itself.

In fall, a number of beetles will often congregate on whitewashed walls and on fenceposts. The insects seem to make a repetition of their "spring flight" and can be taken in numbers.

When killing beetles, it is sometimes better to use alcohol than a cyanide jar. The fumes of the latter change the colors of some beetles, especially those which have brilliant red or yellow markings. The alcohol will not alter the hues unless the insects are left in the bottle too long. A small funnel will be found a help in getting lively beetles into the bottle.

All in all, beetle-hunting is the best of all insect collecting so far as finding specimens is concerned. Beetles are everywhere. There are so many kinds, you are likely to get new species on every trip. And the places where they live are so varied, you will find new adventures in new places whenever you collect members of this largest of the insect tribes.

Chapter VI

BUTTERFLIES AND MOTHS

BOTH butterflies and moths wear coats of colored dust. When you handle one of these creatures, you probably have noticed, your fingers soon become covered with the particles. If you look through a powerful microscope, you will see they are tiny, flattened scales which cover the wings, overlapping like shingles. These "butterfly feathers" often give the insects their brilliant hues and patterns. They also give them the name of the order to which they belong: the Lepidoptera (Lep'-i-dop'-tera). The word means scaly-winged. Only the butterflies and moths, of all the insects, have such scales.

Sometimes, you may find it hard to distinguish the butterflies from the moths. In general, the following rules hold true: Moths have feathery antennae; butterflies smooth and knobbed antennae. When at rest, moths hold their wings out horizontally; butterflies hold their wings vertically above their bodies. Moths have thicker and more wedge-shaped bodies than butterflies. Probably the simplest guide of all is the time of day when you see the insects on the wing. Butterflies are abroad during the day; moths, with a few exceptions, fly at dusk or after dark.

That is the reason we are more familiar with the 700 species of butterflies found in the United States than we are with the 8,800 species of moths. We are awake when the butterflies are afield, asleep when the moths are active.

The biggest and most striking of the 8,800 night insects are the giant silkworm moths, the Cecropia, Io, Promethea, Polyphemus and Luna. With velvety wings that sometimes have a span of nearly half a foot, they are among the most beautiful creatures in the world. The Io is decorated with great round eye-spots and has brilliant red and yellow wings. The Luna is pale green with two flowing, ribbon-like tails. But it is the Polyphemus, with its delicate shadings of brown and pearl, blue and yellow, that is the prize of any collection.

None of these beautiful creatures ever eats. They come from the cocoon, fly about in the darkness, mate, and, at the end of a few days, die. The female leaves behind eggs deposited on the leaves of the trees or plants which form the food of the larvae. These caterpillars feed until they are full grown. Then they spin their cocoons and within these houses of silk turn into pupae. The following spring, they appear as great, brilliant-colored moths and the cycle is complete.

By collecting the cocoons each winter, I am able to watch these gorgeous insects emerge in the spring. Early May is always a time of adventure and excitement when you have made a collection of cocoons. If you live in a large city and cannot find them yourself, you can obtain cocoons from a butterfly supply house. The price usually runs from a dime to a quarter apiece.

A number of moths come from naked pupae made. in the ground instead of from pupae enclosed in the silk of cocoons. When the common tomato worm, for example, reaches its full growth, it burrows into the dirt and there becomes a pupa instead of spinning a cocoon above ground as does the larva of the Luna and the Polyphemus. If you dig around the base of a tree in the late fall, you can often unearth chrysalises. Those of the Hawk moth have curious "jug handles" at one end. These are the curving tube-like cases which hold the long tongues of the developing insects. Such moths have tongues longer than their bodies. On hot summer evenings, you will see them hovering about flowers like hummingbirds, sipping nectar while on the wing.

Not many people take time to watch caterpillars. But if you study these children of the Lepidoptera, you will find they are interesting creatures with curious habits. Knowing the caterpillars, as well as the butterflies and moths which they become, is part of the fun of insect exploring. Any of these lowly creatures will repay watching.

The Woolly Bear caterpillar, for instance, is an insect porcupine. It protects itself by curling up with its bristles pointing in all directions. The Polyphemus larva rears up and clicks its jaws to frighten away its enemies. "Elephant Worms," the caterpillars of the Tiger Swallowtail, have two staring eye-spots on the swollen foreparts of their bodies. Birds, mistaking them for the heads of green snakes, fly away in alarm. The larvae which become Monarch butterflies are equipped with four whips, two in front and two behind. When alarmed by the approach of an enemy, they lash these whips about to scare away the intruder.

The only caterpillar I know that eats meat instead of leaves is the larva of the Wanderer. A curious fact about this little butterfly is that although called the Wanderer, it rarely travels more than a few yards from the bush where it is born. It lives among alder bushes and its caterpillars feast on the white woolly aphides which live in masses on the alder stems. When this larva turns into a pupa, the case which encloses it is marked almost exactly like the face of a monkey!

Another curious caterpillar is the larva of the Abbott's Sphinx. It is able to produce a squeaking noise. How it does it, nobody knows. Sphinx moths, incidentally, get their names from the habit of their caterpillars which rest with their heads drawn in and the front segments of their bodies elevated until they resemble brooding sphinxes.

Most caterpillars eat only one kind of leaves. They will starve to death if given the wrong kind of food. Those of the Regal Fritillary, for example, dine only on violet leaves. A great exception to the rule is the Gypsy Moth. Its caterpillars are known to feed on 500 different plants.

The first butterfly you are likely to see in spring is the Mourning Cloak. It is one of the few insects that hibernate through the winter. It sleeps in hollow trees or crannies and comes out to flit about open glades in February and March when the sun is bright. Its larvae feed largely on poplar trees. Years ago, pioneer settlers in the Middle West used to think these caterpillars were poisonous and they cut down poplar groves where they were found.

Two butterflies you soon will learn to recognize are the Monarch, or Milkweed butterfly, and its "look alike," the Viceroy. Birds shun the Monarch because it exudes a nauseating fluid. By having almost identical black and orange markings, the Viceroy, which has no disagreeable taste and which belongs to an entirely different family, likewise escapes from the attack of birds.

Strange as it seems, butterflies and moths lead dangerous lives. Birds are watching for them in the air; rodents devour them on the ground; spiders snare them among the bushes; dragonflies capture them on the wing.

Probably the biggest butterfly you will capture will be the Tiger Swallowtail. If you live in the Southern states, you may encounter the Giant Swallowtail, which stretches as much as five and a half inches from wingtip to wingtip. If you want to capture the world's biggest butterfly, however, you will have to journey to Africa. On the West Coast of that continent there lives a swallowtail with wings a foot from tip to tip. The tiniest butterflies we have in North America are the midget metal marks and blues. Their wingspread is barely half an inch.

The condensed biography of one butterfly will show us how these insects grow and change and reach the form in which we know them best. Perhaps you can catch females and see them lay their eggs and then watch the caterpillars hatch out, grow and become chrysalises and in the end emerge as butterflies. Here is the life story of the common Black Swallowtail:

On leaves of carrot, parsnip or parsley, the female butterfly deposits her eggs. Each looks like a tiny drop of honey. Centuries ago, when the Roman naturalist, Pliny, was writing his books, he concluded that butterfly eggs were solidified drops of dew. Oftentimes, they look exactly like that. At the end of ten days, the honey-colored "dew drops" of the black swallowtail have turned dark, almost coal black. From them, come spiny little caterpillars. The first thing they do is devour the shells of the eggs from which they hatched. Then they fall to on the juicy leaves to which the eggs were attached.

As they grow, they molt, or shed their skin, from time to time. With each molt, they change their size and coloring. In the end, they have become the familiar green, black and yellow carrot worm. If you poke a finger at them, they defend themselves in a curious manner. They thrust out brilliant orange horns which give off a disagreeable smell.

The full-grown carrot worm is about two inches long. One day, if you are lucky, you will see it spin a button of silk and attach its tail to some solid support in a sheltered spot. Then it makes a loop of silk which it attaches to the same support. Thrusting its head inside the loop, it leans back like a linesman on a telephone pole. In this position, you see it shiver from time to time as a miraculous change comes over it. The skin splits down the back and the soft, pale-green pupa emerges, twisting back and forth until the skin falls away completely. As the chrysalis hardens, it alters its color, usually becoming grayish, dark green or tan. It has been observed that a chrysalis formed with green leaves around it is greenish to match the surroundings while one attached to a board fence or a weathered weed is usually grayish in hue.

Within the shell of the hardened chrysalis, the materials which formed the body of the caterpillar are altered into the structure of the butterfly. One day, weeks later, the upper end of the chrysalis breaks open and the wet and crumpled insect comes forth. It clings motionless while gravity pulls down the unfolding wings which quickly dry and harden. Half an hour or so later, the swallowtail soars away in the sunshine, searching for nectar. Adult butterflies and moths never eat leaves. Only the caterpillars devour foliage. The adults live entirely on liquids, sipping nectar from flowers through their proboscis, a tube which is carried coiled up like a watchspring when it is not in use.

That, in general, is the life story of all butterflies. Some of the moths have a harder time breaking from the silken cocoons within which they pupate. A few are provided with a dissolving fluid which they eject from their mouths to soften the silk at one end of the cocoon when they are ready to emerge.

You won't watch butterflies very long before you see a surprising thing: a butterfly battle. The males of many species engage in duels in the air. They dart, swerve, dash at each other and sometimes even buffet their wings until they are in shreds. The Buckeye, the Pearl Crescent, the Red Admiral, and even the tiny American Copper, are famous as aerial pugilists. Day after day, I once saw the same Red Admiral defending a little stretch of bare ground. At the end of a week, it was still launching out to drive off any other butterfly that ventured near. It put to flight Monarchs many times its size.

Another curious feature of butterfly life requires a sharp nose to appreciate. Some of these insects give off faint odors and perfumes, probably to guide their mates to them. Males seem to give off more pleasing odors than females. A male Monarch, for example, has little packets of scent scales on its hind wings which exude a smell sometimes described as resembling the perfume of red clover blossoms; the females have a cockroach-like odor. The males of one of the swallow-tail butterflies are said to give off a perfume like that of fresh honey, while their mates, the females, produce a vinegary scent.

Of all the insects, the butterflies and moths are probably the most beautiful and attractive. They are easily seen and caught. And their life-habits are intensely interesting. In a book of this scope, it is impossible to give you detailed descriptions of the different butterflies and moths you will meet. Other specialized volumes, some given at the end of this book, will help you as you progress. Your local library should have one or more of these reference books available.

As you go along, make it a habit to look up everything you can find about any new butterfly or moth you capture. It will make your collection more interesting and at the same time will suggest things to watch for when you stalk the insects in the open fields. Almost every insect has little peculiarities of its own.

For example, if you see a Least Skipper, notice if possible, the curious manner in which it moves its antennae in small circles when at rest. The next time you meet a Red Spotted Purple, or Black Admiral, see if you can catch it rubbing its front legs together to produce a faint squeaking sound, one of the strangest musical concerts in the world. The more you learn about butterflies, the more of these curious habits you are on the alert to see.

No matter where you travel, you are likely to find colorful butterflies around you. In 1881, survivors of the wreck of the *Jeannette* came upon a butterfly on the polar ice 700 miles north of the Arctic Circle! However, you can begin your collecting in any backyard garden. Within a mile of your home, the chances are, you will find a surprising variety of these insect beauties. The how and the where of hunting butterflies and moths will be given in the following chapter.

Chapter VII

HOW TO COLLECT BUTTERFLIES
AND MOTHS

WHEN you start on a butterfly hunt, the unexpected often adds to your fun. I remember once stalking a white cabbage butterfly, getting closer and closer until I was within arm's length of the plant on which it rested. Very slowly, I moved my hand toward the insect, watching to see how close I could get before it took alarm. It made not the slightest movement until I actually touched it. Then, it fell over on its side. It was dead. A small white crab spider, which had been holding it, scurried away. The spider, lurking among the leaves, had captured the butterfly as it alighted and had drained away its vital juices.

Most butterflies can be approached best when they are feeding and especially during the first few days after they come from the chrysalises. Sometimes, when Monarchs are absorbed in drinking nectar from milkweeds, you can catch them between a thumb and forefinger, they are so oblivious to what is going on around them.

The best days for butterfly hunting are clear, still ones when the sun is its brightest. Cool days, cloudy

A Luna Moth soon after emerging from its cocoon.
(*See page* 56)

The face of a Praying Mantis.

(*See page* 116)

"What a curious specimen!" said the Katydid.
(*See page 203*)

Japanese Beetles attacking a rose.
(See page 24)

Hunting Beetles in the bark of an apple tree.
(*See page* 51)

A Ladybird Beetle hunting for food on a newly unfolded grape leaf
(See page 42)

Head of a painted beauty Butterfly.
(*See page* 62)

Eye-like spots on this caterpillar of the Tiger Swallowtail butterfly help
scare away birds.

(See page 59)

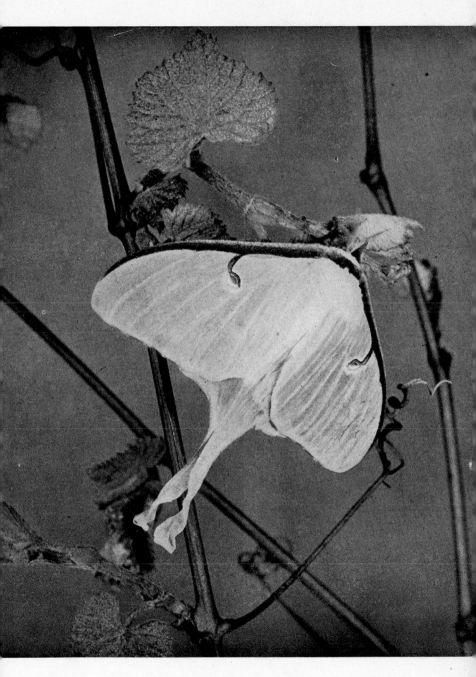

A Luna Moth on a grapevine.
(*See page* 56)

A queer Butterfly Collector—the Praying Mantis with a captured Monarch.
(See page 58)

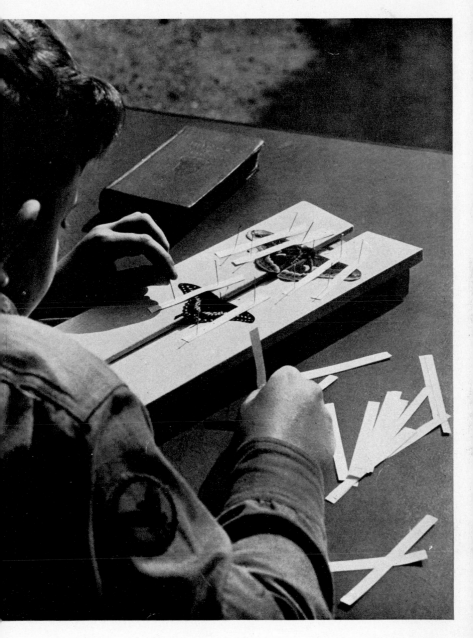

Mounting specimens on a setting board.
(See page 77)

An Ant in the midst of its Aphis "Cattle."
(*See page* 91)

The Lacewing Fly. Its children devour the "cattle" of the Ants.
(*See page* 187)

Termites dined on this piece of wood.
(See page 107)

A Praying Mantis climbing a gladiolus stalk in search of insect prey.
(*See page* 118)

A Hornet's nest cut open to show the hundreds of cells inside.
(*See page 121*)

days, and windy days are usually bad times for collecting. On a morning after an evening thunderstorm, you find some of the most perfect specimens. The storm is thought to kill off old and ragged butterflies and to produce the right atmospheric conditions to enable the new insects to break from their chrysalises.

For all-around hunting, the best places are weedlots bordering woods, clover fields on sheltered hillsides and open stretches where thistles, milkweed, and orange butterflyweed are abundant. As you probably have noticed, the common blue buddleia, or butterfly bush, attracts these gaily colored insects in large numbers.

Just as it takes practice to pitch a curve or ride a bicycle, so it takes practice to gain skill with a butterfly net. In the movies, butterfly collectors always dash madly across a meadow flailing the air with their nets. In real life, the skillful insect-hunter stalks his prey and uses his brains instead of his feet.

When you approach a butterfly, have the sun to one side or in front of you. If it is at your back, it will cast your shadow ahead and may frighten the insect before you are within reaching distance. In most cases, when catching a butterfly, you give a quick sidewise swoop and then, with a twist of your wrist, turn the net so the bag folds over the hoop, imprisoning the creature within. If possible, try to keep from knocking the flowers from the plants in making the swoop. Those which rise above their fellows in a field are a favorite resting place of the butterflies and where you catch one, you may catch another, if you leave the plant undamaged.

Part of the fun of butterfly hunting is learning the habits of the insects so you know where to find them, what sort of flowers each prefers and what they will do when startled. When the Monarch is surprised, it leaps straight up into the air. Consequently it is best to aim the net just above the flower as shown in Fig. 8. The Royal Fritillary, on the other hand, does ex-

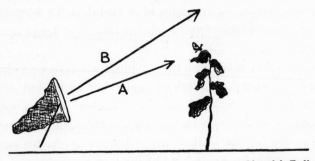

Fig. 8.—In Catching a Monarch, the Net Should Follow the Line B, Instead of A.

actly the opposite. When it is frightened, it drops into the grass and weeds. Knowing what the quarry will do when startled, aids you in handling your net. Insects that rest on the ground, are caught by clapping the net down over them rather than by making a side sweep.

On your first trips afield, you will be out for any game that comes to your net. But, later on, as your collection grows, you will find yourself hunting particular butterflies to fill in gaps. Here is where knowledge of the habits and haunts of the different species will aid you most of all.

The tiny Tailed Blue, for example, shows a marked preference for white flowers. The Black Swallowtails have a peculiarity in connection with the places where they are found in rolling country. The males are encountered most frequently on hilltops, the females in valleys. Some butterflies, like the Grayling, or Wood Nymph, haunt shady roads and paths through woodlands. Others, like the Orange Sulphur, or Puddle Butterfly, disappear as soon as the sun is obscured. These insects are found, oftentimes, in clusters, basking in the midday heat and sipping moisture from the mud of roadside pools. Such facts, stored up in your mind, will help guide you in your hunting.

A friend of mine sometimes used to capture butterflies without a net by using a peculiar method of his own. He would stalk a desired specimen and when close would throw gasoline over it from a small cup. The gasoline killed the insect instantly and my friend maintained that he was able to approach much closer this way than when he was using a net. The plan had one serious drawback in addition to the cost of the gasoline. The insects, covered with the fluid, turned dark temporarily and dropped into the grass where they were difficult to find.

On one occasion, he sighted a freak fritillary with the underside of its wings pure silver. For five minutes he inched his way closer until he was able to throw the gasoline. The butterfly dropped into a tangle of vegetation. Afraid of damaging it, my friend carefully pulled up each blade and weed stalk until he came to his prize!

Instead of stalking butterflies, sometimes you can make them come to you. This is done by setting out baits to attract them. And here you are due for a shock. The best lures for these dainty creatures are not honey and flowers but carrion and rotting fruit! A dead snake, hung up in an open glade, is one of the finest baits of all. It will attract high-fliers, like the Tawny Emperor and the Hackberry Butterfly, which ordinarily are difficult to catch. Among the fruits, fermenting grapes and decaying apples prove most effective. Many species of butterflies will feed on such fruits until they are intoxicated and can be captured with ease. Mash up the spoiled fruit and place it in little piles on the tops of fence-posts and stumps in good "butterfly country," visiting the spots with your net from time to time.

Several butterflies, like the Tiger Swallowtails, sometimes can be attracted by decoys. Cut out an imitation butterfly and paint it with natural colors and set it fluttering in the breeze at the end of a thread. The real insects will often dart down as they pass overhead, circling around the decoy for minutes at a time, held by curiosity.

Night-flying moths can be lured within reach of your net by "sugaring" the trunks of trees. Two baits of the kind that are effective and easy to prepare, consist of peaches—which have been put through a sieve and allowed to ferment and then mixed with white sugar—and fermented bananas and dried apricots mixed with brown sugar.

Mix up about half a pailful of the sweetening and the fermenting fruit. Then about dusk, set out with the pail and a stiff paintbrush. On the lee sides of several tree trunks, paint long streaks of the sweet fluid. It is a good idea to pick trees on the edge of a woods or near a wooded area and to select half a dozen that roughly form a circle. Then, after dark, you can make the rounds with your net and flashlight. A wide variety of moths will oftentimes be found clustered about the streaks dining on the sugary fluid. During the daytime, butterflies and other insects visit the baited trees so you can work these "insect mines" both day and night. "Sugaring" is most effective in spring and fall but can be practiced anytime from March to November.

W. J. Holland, the noted collector of moths and butterflies, tells of an exciting adventure connected with sugaring which nearly ended his insect-hunting career. He was making his rounds, after he had painted several trunks in the dark, when someone began firing at him with a revolver. He discovered the next morning that he had painted one tree just back of a chicken coop. The owner, seeing his flashlight late at night, mistook him for a chicken thief! Moral: choose trees as far as possible from chicken coops and barnyards when you sugar the trunks.

Some moths are active during the early hours of

the night, others during the later hours. So make your rounds at different times. You will find that dark nights with a sultry, almost stormy, atmosphere are best. Beautiful nights, when the moon is its brightest, are the least productive for the moth hunter.

Another trick you can use in collecting the night insects is what is called "assembling." In the spring, when your cocoons begin to hatch, one or more of the moths that appear will be females. Place one of these insects, before it has mated, in a jar with a wire screen cover. When this jar is left in an open space at dusk, males for miles around are likely to be attracted to it, drawn by the faint perfume exuded by the female. They will flutter about the jar, alighting and walking around and around, placing themselves within easy reach of your net.

"Working the lights" is another night sport which provides fun for the moth collector. By using a long-handled net, you can scoop up the insects as they circle about street lamps, especially in parks and on the edge of town. Nets are sometimes made especially for this kind of work. They have jointed handles so they can be shortened or lengthened as desired.

An ordinary net is satisfactory if you use a lantern, the headlights of an automobile, or a porch lamp for your attracting light. By placing a white sheet in front of a lantern or the headlights of a car, you can get the night-fliers to alight upon it. They walk about, charmed by the light, and you can collect them with ease. This form of night activity is likely to yield the best results on the edge of a wood or near a swamp.

In conclusion, let me repeat a bit of advice on how to keep the specimens you capture from being damaged. When you remove a moth or butterfly from the killing jar, use tweezers or pick the insect up by its legs. This will eliminate the danger of rubbing off the dust-like scales. Many otherwise beautiful displays are ruined because the wings of the lepidoptera are dulled and damaged from handling.

Chapter VIII

ORGANIZING YOUR COLLECTION

AT FIRST, you can store your butterflies and beetles in odd boxes and cartons. But, when you begin to capture choice specimens, you will need better housing for them. Also, as your collection grows, you will want to unscramble it and bring order out of chaos by putting the insects of each order and family together.

From such supply houses as Ward's Natural Science Establishment, in Rochester, N. Y., and the General Biological Supply House, in Chicago, Ill., you can purchase ready-made boxes in which to store your specimens. They are rather expensive, costing between two and three dollars for a box nine by thirteen inches, so the chances are you will want to make your own. Paper boxes are not satisfactory as they absorb moisture and cause the specimens to mold. Red cedar should not be used for insect boxes as the resin often oozes out and makes the mounted specimens greasy. White pine or similar wood is best.

Whatever size you make your boxes, you will have to line the bottoms with some material in which you can stick the mounting pins. Sheet cork is best. Balsa wood is satisfactory. If you live on a farm, you can cut

the pith of cornstalks into squares and cement them to
the bottom of the box to form a solid layer over which
you can glue a sheet of white paper. Another inexpen-
sive substitute for sheet cork is corrugated paper such
as comes around books or bottles. Two sheets of the
material are placed, one on top of the other, in the
bottom of the box, the corrugations running at right
angles to each other. A third type of home-made
mounting bottom is formed by making a frame the
right size to fit in the box, and over this gluing sheets
of stiff wrapping paper, as shown in Fig. 9. When dry,

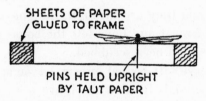

Fig. 9.—Paper, Glued Over Frame, Provides Bottom for
Insect Box.

the frame and the two "drumheads" of paper, are
lowered into the box. The pins, passing through both
sheets of stiff paper, are held upright in position.

Before you put any of these materials in your boxes,
it will be a good idea to bake them in an oven, to kill
any parasites or insect pests which they may contain.
Minute members of the beetle family, called Dermestidae seem to think mounted specimens are insect
beefsteaks laid out especially for them. If you see fine
brown dust collecting under a speciment in a box, you

know the Dermestidae are holding a banquet inside. The remedy is to seal your boxes with binding tape when they are stored away, and to put mothballs or naphthalene inside. By heating the head of a pin, you can push it up into a mothball. When the metal has cooled, pin the pest-chasing chemical in the corner of your box. The best Dermestes insurance of all, is the chemical Dichlorbenzol. It comes in white flakes and can be sprinkled under the cork or other material used at the bottom of the box. However, even Dermestidae have their uses in the world. At one large American museum, I have heard, they are used to clean tiny skeleletons. When they are through, they have consumed every bit of meat and have left the bones as white as though they had been scrubbed.

To preserve soft-bodied insects, larvae and nymphs, seal them in vials filled with eighty per cent alcohol. The eggs of butterflies and moths should be similarly preserved. You can make a holder for such vials by boring holes in a board with a bit just a trifle larger than the diameter of the bottles. Or you can wire or tie the vials in place in your boxes.

If you put cocoons in your collection, to show the different stages of an insect's life history, scald or bake them in order to kill possible parasites. In damp climates, mold is an enemy of insect collections. During long periods of rain, it is a good idea to open your boxes and subject the interiors to moderate heat as a mold preventative.

Common pins are not suitable for mounting speci-

mens. They bend over, they rust and they discolor the
specimens. Special mounting pins, which are thin and
extra strong and treated so they will not rust, should
be used. They cost about thirty-five cents a hundred
and come in several sizes for use in pinning different
insects. You pin your specimens in the boxes in rows
and columns, placing a male and a female together,
and putting insects of the same family in the same box.
Usually, beetles are pinned through the right wing
cover; butterflies and moths through the middle of the
thorax; flies a little to the right of the middle of the
thorax; bugs through the triangle between their wings
on their backs. The correct pinning places are shown
in Fig. 10. Tiny insects are glued on top of the nar-

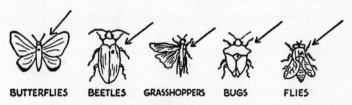

BUTTERFLIES   BEETLES   GRASSHOPPERS   BUGS   FLIES

Fig. 10.—Where to Pin Different Insects.

row end of a little triangle of paper and the pin is
thrust through the wide end. Chrysalises are killed in
alcohol or by chloroform and pinned through the middle for mounting.

When you are collecting butterflies, dragonflies or
other large insects, you can place them in paper triangles for safekeeping until you have time to mount
them. They can even be left in the triangles for weeks

without damage. How to fold these paper containers is shown in Fig. 11. The best paper is light, medium-stiff material. Newspapers can be used in an emergency but the printing on them makes them less desirable. You can fold up several hundred of these triangles during leisure moments and pack them in little bunches with rubber bands around them so they will be ready when you go insect hunting.

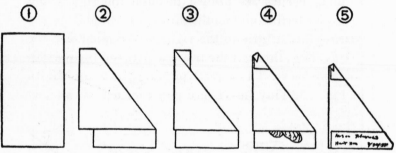

Fig. 11.—How to Fold Paper into Triangles for Holding Insects.

After butterflies have been in the triangles for some time, they become stiff. Before they can be mounted, they have to be softened in a "relaxing box." Any tight metal box or earthenware container holding a layer of wet sand or sawdust so the atmosphere will be very moist inside, will do. Leave the insects sealed inside for from twelve to twenty-four hours. To prevent mold, add a few drops of carbolic acid to the water used in moistening the sand or sawdust. Another method of relaxing specimens is to place them in their triangles between clean towels which have been damped slightly.

When the specimens are sufficiently relaxed, you can move the wings without danger of breaking them off. They are then ready for the setting board where butterflies, moths, dragonflies, grasshoppers and other winged insects are held in the desired position until they have dried. You can place your specimens on the board immediately after you catch them, or you can do this after they have dried in the triangles and have been relaxed again. In the latter case, the insects dry

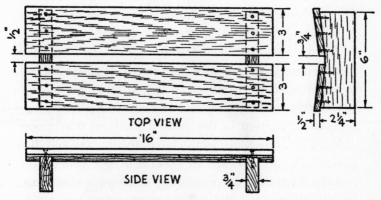

TOP VIEW

SIDE VIEW

Fig. 12.—Details of the Construction of a Setting Board.

much quicker than when they are put on the setting board as soon as they are brought in from the fields.

How the setting board is constructed is shown in Fig. 12. Use soft wood such as white pine for the material. Boards from packing cases are suitable. If you have the center slit wider at one end than at the other, you can place insects having larger bodies at that end and those with smaller bodies at the other end.

Place the butterfly or other insect with the body in the slit and then adjust the wings until they are in their best position, pinning narrow strips of paper or tracing cloth in place to keep them from moving until they are dry. A setting needle, to help with the work of adjusting the wings, can be made by warming wax and pushing the eye-end of a good-sized needle up into the mass which is then pressed into a handle. When the wax is cold, you can hold the needle easily and use it for the delicate work of adjusting the wings of butterflies and moths without rubbing away the scales and thus damaging the specimens.

The insects have to remain on the setting board for several days until they are thoroughly dry. Keep them in a protected place where mice and other pests can't get at them while they are drying. When they are permanently dried in the desired position, the insects can be pinned in place in the boxes for storage and display. Sometimes, heads of specimens get broken off and mounted insects occasionally lose legs or antennae. Supply houses sell special insect glue for cementing such parts back in place. But be careful in such work. Be *sure* you have the right part in the right place. I remember one fearful and wonderful insect I saw displayed in a store window. It had, in tandem, two bodies and eight legs! Several specimens had been dropped on the floor and the various parts had been reassembled with a gluepot and a rough-and-ready idea of insect anatomy.

Because dragonflies often lose their abdomens when

mounted without special precautions, it is an excellent idea to reinforce them before they are placed on the spreading board. This can be done by pushing a stiff piece of horsehair into the body just back of the head until the end comes out at the tip of the abdomen. With sharp shears, snip off both ends of the hair. Inside the insect, the horsehair forms a sort of "backbone" which keeps the dried specimen from falling apart.

In some cases where protective coloration plays an important part in the life of an insect, you can dramatize this fact by mounting your specimens on circles of sand or bark glued in place. Cocoons also sometimes are aided by protective coloration and this can be shown in a similar manner in your collection. The plant foods on which some larvae feed will help make complete your presentation of life cycles. One simple method of preserving plant foods has been reported from England. Cut off a sprig of the plant and stick it in white sand placed in the bottom of a wide-mouthed jar. Then carefully pour in more white sand until the jar is full and the sprig completely covered. Leave the jar in a warm place, such as on a mantelpiece near a fire, for two or three weeks. The sprig then will be found to be dried in natural position. As it is brittle, care must be used in getting it out of the jar. In removing any adhering sand-grains, use a camel's-hair, or soft water-color brush. The sprig is then ready for tying, by loops of thread, to a cardboard mount. If you treat several specimens of food plants in this manner at the same time, be sure to place slips of paper in the different jars telling for which larvae the plants are intended. Otherwise, you may be confused and get the wrong caterpillars on the leaves.

Usually the labels in display boxes are pinned on the left or above the specimens. In the case of the tiny insects glued to paper triangles, the labels and data cards are placed on the same pin, below the specimens. Incidentally, to give a neat appearance to your collection, have all specimens and cards the same height above the bottom.

On your labels give the common and scientific names of your specimen, the place where it was caught, the date, and, when possible, what it was doing when captured. If it was eating, what was it eating? Such information is really valuable and makes your collection far more than merely a cemetery for dead insects. No matter how well you mount your insects, if you have scanty labels or have the specimens wrongly identified, your work will have little permanent value. Of course, you can't identify all the creatures you catch immediately. Doing that is part of the winter fun, when living insects are few and far between. Always when you are not sure of your identification, place a small question mark on the label.

Collectors for the American Museum of Natural History, in New York City, fill in cards for their different specimens which answer such questions as these: Date? Time? Locality? Temperature? Weather—rainy, cloudy, clear, fog? Soil—rock, gravel, sand, clay, humus, mud? Was it moist, medium or dry?

Was the slope level, slight, moderate, steep, cliff? Was the exposure North, East, South or West? What sort of vegetation? Water conditions—stagnant, slight current, swift; Fresh, brackish or salt? How was the insect caught—by hand, sweeping, seine, dredging, sugar, light, trap, sifting or beating? Name of the Collector? Special Remarks.

Each of these Museum field cards has a number. That gives you an idea. If you want to go about this exploring among the insects in a thorough way, you will always carry your little notebook in which to jot down facts about the specimens you catch. Give each important specimen a number and put the same number on the paper triangle into which you slip the insect. Then, later on when you have leisure, you can get insects and facts together and record the information as you mount the specimens.

Chapter IX

THE ANTS

AMONG all the insects, the ants probably come closest to being human. Their ways resemble ours in a surprising number of instances.

They go to war, often marching in columns and attacking in unison. They keep cattle in the form of smaller insects that give off honeydew, milk them regularly, and, in some cases, even build barns to shelter them. Some ants plant fungus gardens and gather crops like farmers. Others harvest grain and store it in granaries. Still others have servants and slaves to wait on them. Many ants keep pets in their homes. In fact, it is said that the ants have domesticated more different kinds of creatures than man has!

Sometimes, tropical ants live in great cities that contain half a million inhabitants. Their nests have been known to occupy as much as three hundred cubic yards of earth. Finally, like man and unlike most insects, ants live for years. Workers have a life span up to seven years and queens have been known to live eighteen years. The same underground cities are sometimes occupied for half a century, one generation of ants "inheriting real estate" from the generation before.

The life of the ant colony begins with the swarming of the queens and males. This usually occurs on some still and sultry day. Sometimes, the flying ants will appear in such numbers they seem to fill the sky. A few years ago, in southern California, so many billions of the winged insects appeared over the Malibu Hills they formed a black cloud which was mistaken for smoke from a forest fire. Rangers rushed to the spot and found the air swarming with the insects.

Certain weather conditions stimulate the ants to make their mating flights. This assists in producing cross-fertilization, as the inmates of many nests of the same kind take to the air at once. There are 3,500 species of ants and none of them mate with other species; all breed only with those of their kind.

The workers, which make up the great bulk of the colony, cannot fly. Only the queens and males have wings. And they use them but once, the time they soar into the sky on their mating flight. The males live only a short time afterwards and as soon as the queens land, they bite or break off the wings they have finished using. Sometimes, they accomplish this by rubbing against weeds or pebbles, sometimes they bite off the wings with their jaws, at other times pull them off with their legs. For the rest of their lives, most of the queens will be voluntary prisoners beneath the ground.

They begin this subterranean existence by digging a little chamber in the soil, or in rotting wood, according to the species. Some tropical ants even build nests of leaves, sewing them together with silken threads. This is accomplished by a curious example of insect child labor. The larvae of these ants secrete a silk-like adhesive. Some of the insects hold the leaves together with legs and jaws while other workers pass the larvae back and forth like living shuttles to bind the leaves together.

Most of the ants we know, make their nests in the ground. After the queens have torn away their wings and dug out a chamber, they begin laying eggs. Out of these hatch soft, translucent, legless grubs. They are shaped like crook-necked gourds. Among the relatives of the ant—the wasps and bees—the young have fixed cradles or cells. But ant babies are moved about, washed, and, as every boy knows, rushed from the underground chambers to a place of safety when the nest is disturbed.

The first grubs that hatch from the eggs are fed with the saliva of the queen. For weeks and even months, the queen is not able to obtain food. She is too busy laying eggs and caring for the grubs. As a hibernating bear lives on its fat, she lives by digesting the tissues of the now-useless wing muscles. Tests have shown that queens can go without food for the greater part of a year and that even workers can live for almost nine months without food.

In other ways, ants can endure astonishing hardships. Members of one species have been revived after being under water for twenty-seven hours; another after being submerged seventy hours; and a third after being without air for eight days! This probably explains how ants nesting in the bed of a dry stream are able to live through sudden floods and freshets. Even more amazing is the vitality of injured ants. In one laboratory, a beheaded ant remained alive for nineteen days and, in another, a worker lived forty-one days after its head was severed from its body. It even continued to walk up until within two days of its death!

Because the first grubs that hatch out receive less food than those which come later, they are usually smaller than the average. As the colony grows, the job of caring for the young is turned over to the workers. Some larvae are equipped with spines and ridges at the base of the jaws. By rubbing them together, they produce a shrill sound which, like the crying of a baby, attracts the attention of the nurses that wash and feed them. In return for their care, the nurses get a fatty secretion which the grubs exude and which the ants relish greatly as food.

As soon as the grubs are full grown, they spin little cocoons for themselves. When you buy "ant eggs" for goldfish or canaries, these cocoons are what you get. In the Black Forest, in Germany, collecting ant cocoons used to be a regular occupation. Millions of the "eggs" were shipped to all parts of the world.

It is within these tiny silken shells that the grubs change into adult ants. Sometimes, they have to be helped from the cocoons by the nurses who bite holes in the little prisons and help the weak inmates out.

Then, like babies, the newborn insects are washed, brushed and fed.

It may take years before a colony becomes well established. Sometimes the queen is killed by fungus in damp soil. But, ordinarily, she is soon able to turn the care of the young over to the workers and to devote herself to laying eggs. This she continues to do year after year. Unlike honeybees, the ant queen feels no hostility toward younger queens. Sometimes, the latter return to the home colony after the mating flight and add their eggs to those of the original queen, thus swelling the population of the insect city.

Among the strangest stories in connection with queen ants is one reported from Tunis, in northern Africa. At the end of her mating flight, this female descends and wanders about in front of the nest of another species. The workers swarm out, capture her, and drag her by the legs and antennae into the nest. Here they try to kill her. But she takes refuge on the back of the larger queen which has founded the colony. She remains for hours in this position. And what do you suppose she is doing? Cutting off the head of her host! By the time the original queen has been decapitated, the invader has acquired the nest odor and is accepted by the workers. They are afterwards kept busy bringing up her offspring. In the end, all the original workers die and the interloper is queen of a flourishing colony of her own kind!

Some queens among the tropical ants are more than a hundred times the size of the workers of the same species. In one instance, the queen is so much larger than her first offspring that she cannot feed them. So, when she leaves on her mating flight, several of the tiny workers cling to her legs and go sailing through the sky with her. When she lands and establishes her colony, they are there to feed and care for the first baby ants that appear from the eggs.

Among the mountains of Switzerland, one species of yellow ant always builds its nest in elongated form running east and west. Mountaineers, lost in the fog, sometimes feel their way along the nests made by these ants, using them like compasses to check up on the direction they are going.

In a few instances, ants of different species live in the same nests. A remarkable example of the kind occurs in South America where a large brown ant and a small dark ant live in the same home. It is a curious ball of earth built around a tree branch and tunneled with interconnecting passages. The outer "apartments" are occupied by the small ants, the inner chambers by the big ones. The insects seem to live together for military advantage. If a small foe attacks the ball of earth, the little ants rush out to defend it. The larger and more formidable ants pour out only when the attack is serious.

Almost all ants will defend their nests against attacks but some of the insects have developed great armies that march long distances and attack insects and even animals they meet in their path. Entirely blind, these uncanny creatures march through the jungles in regular lines. Only the males among the army ants are winged. The females, like the workers, are wingless.

The Amazons, or slave-making ants, also make regular marches to attack neighboring nests and carry away the pupae which they raise up to be their slaves. In one instance, an Amazon colony was watched every day for a month. During that time, it sent out forty-four different expeditions. Sometimes they raided the same nest over and over again until the persecuted ants moved to a new location.

For so many generations have the slave-keeping ants depended upon servants to feed them that they have lost the ability to feed themselves. They will die with food all around them if the slaves are removed. Once, when sugar was placed near a nest of Amazons, the slaves came out and gorged themselves. After a while, the hungry master ants appeared. They tugged at the legs of the slaves, apparently to remind them of their forgotten duty. At once, the smaller ants began feeding drops of food to their masters.

The habit of feeding one another with food which has been swallowed and stored in a "social stomach" is a characteristic of the ants. Most of the food they eat, instead of going directly to their stomachs, is retained in a sort of crop from which they can bring drops to feed other members of the colony. This process is called regurgitation.

Once, a scientist made a test to see how widely a given bit of food would be distributed throughout an ant nest. He dyed some honey bright blue. When an ant swallowed some of the liquid, the blue showed through the sides of its abdomen. When it gave drops to another ant which solicited food, that ant's abdomen also became blue. In the course of time, dozens of ants in the nest were going around with blue showing through the thin walls of their stomachs. All had been fed with regurgitated honey from the original feeding.

Bees live on nectar and pollen, some beetles eat only carrion, termites rarely consume anything but wood. But the ants can live on a wide variety of things. They eat meat, seeds, vegetable matter, honeydew; they are both carnivorous and vegetarian. This has helped them survive. They not only hunt afield for their food but produce it close at hand. Two of the most remarkable examples of "ant husbandry" are the activities of the harvester ants and the leaf-cutting ants.

When King Solomon wrote: "Go to the ant, thou sluggard!" he was thinking of the harvester insects which diligently collect seeds and carefully store them away in underground granaries. These ants bring the grain to the surface and spread it out to dry when the seeds become wet, thus preventing their stores from growing moldy. They also show almost-human intelligence by carefully biting off one end as they carry in the seeds. This keeps them from sprouting in the underground nests!

In some species of harvester ants, the larger soldier insects have the job of "nut crackers" for the colony. They crush the shells of the seeds with their large jaws so the smaller workers can get at the food inside. As many as eighteen different kinds of seeds have been found in the granaries of these provident little creatures. All harvester ants live in semi-arid localities. They store up grain for periods of drought.

Just as pirates swooped down on treasure-laden ships to obtain booty, so ants from one colony will attack the nest of another colony to obtain the stored-up seeds in the granary. Near Philadelphia, Pa., years ago, a battle between neighboring colonies continued for nearly three weeks. In another case, a war between rival harvester ants lasted forty-six days.

So far as is known, these insects never plant seeds to raise crops. But that in effect is what another kind of ant does. These leaf-cutters carry bits of vegetation into their nests and on them plant tiny fungus gardens. When the queen of one of these colonies sets out on her mating flight, she carries a minute bit of fungus stuffed in a special pouch. One of the first things she does after she has located her new home, is to plant the pellet of fungus. Sometimes she even fertilizes it by breaking open her first eggs to provide additional nourishment. Later on, just as farmers spread manure over the fields to fertilize their crops, the ants spread the dung of certain caterpillars over the decaying leaves which form the "soil" for the fungus.

Each species of leaf-cutting ant uses a particular kind of fungus. In some mysterious way, the workers treat the gardens so tiny white swellings appear on the fungus. They resemble minute cabbage heads. It is these that the ants bite off and use for food. Exactly the same fungus has been grown in the laboratory under a wide variety of conditions. But the "cabbages" never appeared. Producing them is the secret of the ants.

Most leaf-cutters live in tropical America and the Southwest. So the chances are you will never have an opportunity to watch these insect farmers at work. But, on almost any summer day, you can observe ant "dairy-hands" tending their herds. Ants are so fond of the sweet honeydew given off by aphides, or plant lice, that Linnaeus, the pioneer naturalist, called the aphis the "milk cows of the ants." For hours ants will stand guard over the aphides, "milking" them from time to time by stroking their backs with their antennae. I have tried stroking the backs of aphides with hairs and blades of fine grass. But the tiny insects knew better than to mistake my heavy touch for the light, tapping stroke of the ant's antennae. The ants know a secret "tap language" we do not.

The "milk" of the aphis is a colorless fluid with a sweetish taste. The manna of the Bible is thought to have been solidified honeydew. In twenty-four hours, a single aphis has been seen to give off as many as forty-eight drops of honeydew, a by-product of the sap which the little insect sucks.

In some regions of the United States ants have become serious pests through their help in spreading the corn-root aphis. They keep the eggs of these insects in their nests over the winter. When spring comes, they plant them on the roots of smartweed until the corn plants are growing strongly. Then they dig down and place the sucking insects on the corn roots. Afterwards, they visit their "cattle" from time to time. In cases where farmers have pulled up the infested plants, ants have been seen wandering about with aphides in their jaws, looking for new homes for their "cows."

A few species of ants construct tiny sheds or barns of leaves to serve as shelters or pens for their cattle. Others keep their insect cows permanently underground. Like creatures which inhabit sunless caves, these aphides become snow-white.

In Southwestern states, the honey ants have devised a curious method of storing up accumulated honeydew and nectar. Certain workers become living casks. They never leave the nests and hang like bloated wine-skins from the ceilings of underground chambers. In their distended bodies they store the honeydew which the workers bring. When droughts occur, the whole colony lives on the fluid stored up in the "honey cask" ants. These sweet and swollen insects are sometimes served as a delicacy at wedding feasts in Mexico.

In the nests of many ants, you will find a great variety of insect "pets" and hangers-on. Tiny little beetles—with strange horns like ribbons, scimitars, drumsticks and antlers springing from their heads— are widely associated with ants. It is believed they are kept for the perfume they give off, a delicate scent their hosts enjoy. Secretions from the glands of one

strange ant-hill beetle have been found to contain pure
iodine. In artificial nests, observers have seen ants
fondle their beetle pets and sometimes carry them
about on their backs for hours at a time.

Tiny crickets, which also inhabit ant nests, are less
welcome. They nibble at the fatty secretions found on
the legs of the ants. When the latter charge at them,
the nimble crickets twist and turn so expertly their
pursuers cannot catch them. The armored bodies of
the ants prevent them from whirling or zigzagging
sharply. They can follow only a straight line or a
sinuous path.

Of all the inmates of the ant hill, probably the least
welcome is a sooty-colored beetle which skulks like a
jackal through the subterranean passages. Five or six
will sometimes corner a lone ant, tear it to pieces and
then fall to quarreling like wolves over the fragments.
Whenever ants see these ravenous creatures, they
charge at them with open jaws. But the beetles are
provided with a curious form of defense. They merely
lift their flexible tails and emit a drop of whitish fluid
which appears to affect the ants much as if a bottle of
ammonia were uncorked in their faces. They start
back and the beetle scurries away to safety.

Another strange foe of the ants is the common
"doodle bug" or ant lion. You have often seen the
tiny craters which it digs in the sands. Hidden at the
bottom, with jaws widespread, it waits for an ant to
stumble into the pit and slide to the bottom. By explosive jerks of its head, the doodle bug digs its pit, going

around and around in narrowing circles. It always walks backward, unable to go forward! Also, this strange creature has a "dead end" stomach. It gets rid of undigested food by spitting it out from time to time.

Altogether, there are something like 2,000 different species of insects that inhabit the nests of ants as guests, tolerated companions or enemies of the colony. Some of these creatures have been living with the ants for millions of years. When Dr. William Morton Wheeler, of Harvard, studied pieces of amber 30,000,-000 years old, he found embedded in the transparent material with ants, aphides and other common guests of the ant communities.

Four hundred years before the birth of Christ, Herodotus, the early historian, wrote of ants that dug gold for princes in India. While these legendary insect miners have never been discovered, ants are known to aid man in many ways. Like earthworms, they bring fresh soil to the surface. Their cocoons provide fish and bird food. When naturalists in the field want small skeletons cleaned, they place them near ant hills and come back to find every bit of meat eaten away and the bones left clean and white. In Mexico, natives place vermin-infested garments over an ant hill and let the members of the colony dine on the lice. Further south, in Brazil, doctors used to employ the heads of large soldier ants as ligatures for closing wounds. After the ants had clamped their jaws on the skin, closing the wound, the physician would snip off the heads and leave them, as a modern doctor leaves stitches, until the wound healed!

Someone has figured out that it would take about 100,000 average-sized ants to weigh as much as a man. Yet these tiny creatures have developed an elaborate insect society. They have established great cities. They have continued their complex way of life for millions of years. The ant belongs to one of the oldest civilizations on earth.

The next time you see winged ants pouring from the ground on a mating and dispersal flight, notice the weather. During the years I have been watching these remarkable creatures, I have never known such a flight to begin except when at least twenty-four hours of calm and settled weather followed. But how can the ants predict what weather lies ahead? Nobody is sure. Their ability as weather prophets is one of the many mysteries connected with ant-life. One afternoon in the fall of 1951, a swarm of winged red ants issued from the ground near my backdoor. At the time, the sky was dark and threatening. Never before had I seen male and female ants appear under such conditions. I thought their instinctive wisdom must have gone astray. But I was wrong. Fifteen minutes later, every ant was hurrying back into its underground tunnel. The exodus had been delayed for another day and better weather.

Chapter X

HOW TO BUILD AN ANT HOUSE

IN THE last chapter, we made the acquaintance of the ants and witnessed some of their amazing abilities and habits. In this chapter, we will learn how we can become even more intimately acquainted with them by building a transparent house in which we can watch them at work.

Of course, we won't see all the wonders reported in the preceding pages because they cover the whole world of ants. But we will see the insects building their underground nests, feeding each other, placing their dead in cemeteries and doing the thousand and one tasks which make up the activity of the ant hill.

Building a vertical "glass sandwich," which enables us to see all these things, is comparatively easy. The materials you will need are few and they are not expensive. Here is the list:

Two pieces of clear window glass, 12″ by 18″.
Two sticks of white pine, 21″ long, 2″ wide and 1½″ high.
Two sticks of white pine, 15″ long, 2″ wide and 1½″ high.
Two pieces of heavier wood, such as oak, 6″ long, 2½″ wide and 1″ thick.
One roll of heavy white adhesive tape.

The first step in making your ant house will be to cut two grooves, $\frac{1}{2}''$ deep and a trifle wider than the thickness of your panes of glass, running lengthwise down the white pine sticks, as shown in Fig. 13. Each groove should be cut $\frac{5}{8}''$ in from the edge of the stick.

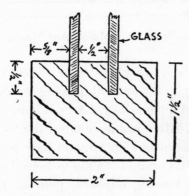

Fig. 13.—How Glass Panes Are Sunk in Strips of the Frame of the Ant House.

Next, place the sticks in a miter box and saw off the ends at a forty-five-degree angle, slanting in toward the grooved sides. Thus, you will have a frame with grooves into which the two panes of glass will slip, with approximately $\frac{1}{2}''$ of space between. The hardest part of the job is over.

Now, take the $6''$ by $2\frac{1}{2}''$ wooden blocks and cut them as shown in Fig. 14. They will form the feet on which the upright glass sandwich will rest without tipping over. It is now time to hunt the inmates that will live in your ant house. The common brown ants,

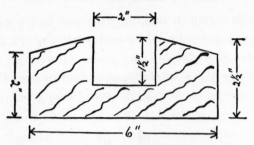

Fig. 14.—Foot for Holding Ant House Upright.

found in almost every garden or vacant lot, are satisfactory. Dig up the ant hill, placing the dirt as well as the insects in a paper bag. Carry it home with the top tightly shut. After you have taped the bottom of your frame, as shown in Fig. 15, and have placed a string or rubber band around the top to keep the sides of the frame from moving outward, pour in the ants and

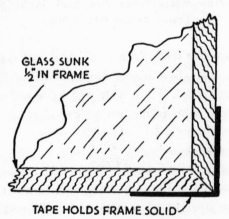

GLASS SUNK
½" IN FRAME

TAPE HOLDS FRAME SOLID

Fig. 15.—Detail of Ant House, Showing How Tape
Holds the Corners Solid.

dirt until the space between the panes of glass is filled about two-thirds of the way to the top. Then, after you have bored two small air-holes through the top stick of the frame, slip it in place and tape the corners. When the house is placed on the two feet, it stands upright as shown in Fig. 16, and you are ready for the fun of watching your captives settle down to house-keeping in their new home.

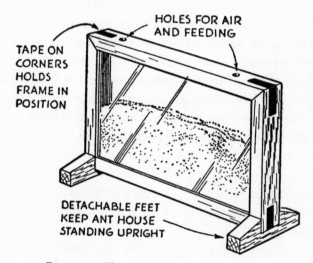

HOLES FOR AIR AND FEEDING

TAPE ON CORNERS HOLDS FRAME IN POSITION

DETACHABLE FEET KEEP ANT HOUSE STANDING UPRIGHT

Fig. 16.—The Ant House Complete.

There are many other ways of building an ant house, but this one requires little skill with tools and it can be taken apart easily. You can paint the frame if you desire to make it more attractive. When you wish to feed or water your ants you can do this by removing one of the adhesive strips at an upper corner and tilting the top strip upward. Or, you can use a medicine dropper and insert it through the air holes at the top.

Don't overfeed your ants. A drop or two of honey or molasses will keep a fairly large colony supplied for days. Solid food should be inserted only in tiny morsels. Bits of mashed walnuts, tiny pieces of spongecake dipped in honey, fragments of apples and bananas, as well as pieces of dead insects, are all welcomed by the inmates of an ant house. Because the ants require a fairly moist soil for their surroundings, dampen the dirt by inserting water at least once a week. Don't keep your ant house near a radiator or in the bright sunshine. If there is much tobacco smoke in the room where the ants are kept, they will not thrive.

By observing these simple rules, you will give your insect guests a chance to live normally. One other thing: When you dig up the ants always try to get a queen along with the workers. Otherwise, your colony will show you only part of the wonders of the ant city.

As soon as your insects are in their new home, your fun begins. The ants will start digging furiously in the soil, excavating a small tunnel which they enlarge into a general assembly hall or a chamber for the queen. Until this is accomplished, the insects are likely to work day and night. The queen will be seen carrying particles to the surface which are too large for the workers to handle. When the hall is completed, however, the queen ceases work and remains in the chamber. The other ants begin digging tunnels away from this central hall, part going one way and part the other. When they strike the sides of the ant house, they head down; when they reach the bottom, they head across it. Finally, both groups of workers meet, like men boring a tunnel from opposite sides of a river. Then, the workers begin excavating branches from the tunnels they have established. In the end, the interior of your "sandwich" observatory will be honeycombed with underground passages.

Even in the early stages of the life of your ant colony, you will see surprising things, such as the distribution of labor. How does each ant know what it is supposed to do? Years ago, Lord Avebury, in England, put little daubs of paint on the backs of different ants in his observation nest so he could tell the insects apart. For three months, he made hourly notes each day on what the various ants were doing.

Day after day, he found, the same workers were performing the same tasks. He noted that the identical three ants came every day to carry back the honey which was placed in the ant house. They, apparently, were the food-providers. Avebury removed one of these insects from the nest. Another ant took its place and continued making regular trips to and from the honey. He imprisoned this one. Another ant took over its duties.

Who gave these ants their instructions? How did these particular insects know the definite assignment they were supposed to carry out? We can only guess.

Part of the fascination we get in watching the ants is the feeling that we are exploring the unknown.

It will not be long, after your nest is established, before there will be one or more deaths in the colony. You will see the corpses carefully removed to some spot, usually on top of the soil and far in one corner of the nest. This will be the cemetery of the colony. Afterwards all dead ants will be deposited in the same spot. Sometimes, before such a cemetery has been established, one of the workers in a nest will wander about for hours with a dead ant in its jaws, seeking the right place to put it.

Cleanliness is a characteristic of the ants. You will see the same worker wash itself fifteen or twenty times a day. Frequently, they help each other with their toilet. The insects co-operate in other ways, too. Numerous stories are told of the manner in which they bridge obstacles under natural conditions. One experimenter separated some ants from their nests with a line of glue while they were tending their aphis cattle. He reported that the insect herdsmen picked up their cows and tossed them into the sticky fluid to make a bridge over which they walked in safety! On other occasions, the insects have been seen casting pellets of dirt into sticky fly paper which was in their line of march.

Some years ago, a scientist put a thin line of water around some of the ants' pupae. He saw the insects cast dirt into the water until they could walk across and get their immature young. It seemed such an amazing example of insect intelligence that he repeated the experiment without putting any of the young ants inside the circle of fluid. Again, the ants made a bridge just as they had before! Casting dirt into water or other fluid seems to be a reflex action rather than a sign of thought on the part of the ants. In the nests, the insects cover over damp spots and outside they had carried out the same procedure.

Other instances of apparent intelligence are harder to explain. Thirty years ago, Miss A. M. Fielde, one of the pioneer American ant observers, reported how the insects in one of her nests solved a problem of life and death. The immature ants in her brood chambers could not stand the ultra-violet light in sunshine. So, during the day, she spread a cloth over the chamber to darken it. Once, she left the cover off. The worker ants pasted a thin layer of dirt all over the underside of the glass to form a curtain. Miss Fielde scraped off this dirt. The next day, it was back again. The ants had spent the whole night replacing it!

Yet, you will see these insects, which are so sagacious at one time, fail entirely to solve a simple problem another time. Honey has been placed where it was a fraction of an inch beyond their reach in a nest. Although their lives depended upon it and there was plenty of dirt all around them, the insects never thought of building a mound an eighth of an inch high in order to reach the food.

As the days go by, you will find that the insects you are observing within their glass house, sleep just as we do. Even during the daytime, ants occasionally will lie down in a depression, pull their legs close to their bodies and go to sleep. You can sometimes stroke them with a straw without awakening them. But, if you rap the nest sharply, they will jump up at once. One observer tested out different kinds of ants and found the soldiers sleep longer and more soundly than the smaller workers. As they awaken, ants will often stretch their legs and even open their jaws as though they were yawning.

Although nobody knows exactly how they do it, ants seem to have an elaborate system of communication. You will see the insects, standing head to head, twiddling their antennae in a sort of deaf-and-dumb language. That the tiny creatures can "talk" well enough to convey ideas, can be proved in your observation house. After you have placed the legs of the table, on which the house is resting, in saucers of water to keep the insects from escaping, remove the top of the glass sandwich and tip the nest over on its side to let the ants wander about the table. Then place a piece of meat or a dead insect in a far corner of the table. Sooner or later, one of the roving worker ants will find it. Then watch closely. The food will be too big for him to transport home. So, he starts on the run for help, returning with others equally excited. He has "told" of his find so clearly that the other ants understand him.

To help you see interesting things that go on inside

the transparent walls of your ant house, you can attach a magnifying glass to the outside. A simple method of doing this is by means of a heavy rubber band and a string. The rubber will stretch so the glass can be secured in any desired position for observing special activity within the nest.

Some watchers of ants report that the insects engage in various forms of play, wrestling like puppies and racing about in games of tag. However, their ways are so strange, it is often hard to say just what they are doing and we must be careful in ascribing motives for their actions. Seeing their astonishing activity, is, in itself, sufficiently amazing. So much remains to be learned about these insects that if you spend enough time observing your "cross-section nest," you are sure to witness things that will surprise and puzzle you.

Miss Fielde tells of one instance of the sort. She dropped an ant from a strange colony into one of her nests to see what would happen. Ordinarily, the intruder would have been killed at once. In this case, however, the workers about it seemed hypnotized. They swayed back and forth rhythmically, rooted to the ground. The intruder passed among them half a dozen times without being molested. A worker which had not been present when the strange ant was dropped into the nest, came from another compartment. It tapped and butted one of the "hypnotized" insects but the latter showed no sign of recognition. As long as Miss Fielde watched, the stranger paraded in front of the swaying ants and they made no move to harm it. Some puzzling, mysterious effect had been produced by the ant from the other colony.

It is the unexplained things about these insects that make watching them such an interesting adventure. We realize that, within a few inches of our noses, there is another world in which the customs and abilities of the inhabitants are so remote from our own that often-times we can only guess at what is occurring before us.

Chapter XI

THE TERMITES

A FRIEND of mine, one day, looked out a back window and saw his grape arbor lying flat on the ground. Termites had consumed so much of the wood of the framework that the arbor had collapsed of its own weight. Another friend leaned against a flagpole and the timber swayed like a straw in a breeze. A large part of the interior wood had been devoured by the insects. The annual food bill of termites throughout the United States is estimated at $40,000,000.

Yet, these insects can't eat wood. That is, they can't by themselves. One of the strangest partnerships in nature enables them to do it. A host of tiny one-celled animals live in their intestines and break down the cellulose into digestible substances. When the insects are placed under high temperatures or are treated with oxygen under pressure, all these little partners die. The termites go on chewing and swallowing wood. But they can't get any nourishment from it. They soon waste away and die of starvation. During the first twenty-four hours of their lives, baby termites lack these internal helpers and have to be fed predigested food by the older insects. Only through the aid of the flocks of smaller creatures that exist within their bodies can the termites live.

This is only one of many curious facts about the so-called "white ants." In the first place, they are not ants and in the second place they are rarely white. They belong to the Isoptera, (I-sop'-tera) an entirely different order of insects from that which includes the true ants. They are more nearly related to the roaches. Almost always, the ants and the termites are at war; the ants attacking and the termites defending their nests. One curious kind of soldier termites, called the nasuti or nosey ones, have long projecting snouts from which they eject a glue-like fluid which immediately hardens. In battle, they aim for the thin stalk connecting the ant's head and body. When this is gummed up, the ant is unable to turn and bite and is kept so occupied trying to "ungum" itself that it can no longer take part in the attack.

Another form of termite soldier has a head which is enlarged and coated with a heavy bone-like covering. The rest of its body is soft. When the galleries of the termites are attacked, these big-headed creatures rush to the doorways and thrust their hard heads into the openings, filling them and blocking the passages to invaders.

Termites are among the longest-lived of all the insects. More than that, in some species, the king and queen of a colony stay mated throughout their lives. Records show that two of these insects lived as mates in an observation nest for twenty-five years—approximately the length of a human generation. The old queens become shrunken and wrinkled. Yet, they keep on laying eggs, like automatic machines, one every few seconds, up to an advanced age. As noted before, it is estimated that some termites lay as many as 10,000,000 eggs during their lifetime. One African queen termite has a bloated, egg-filled body so large she cannot move it about. She resembles a great gray-white sausage nearly four inches long. The king, her mate, is only 1-160th her size and she has 2,400 times the bulk of one of the workers which surround her.

The life of the colony starts like that of the ants and bees with a flight of the winged males and females. But, unlike the others, its purpose is not for mating, but for spreading out and establishing new colonies. Before the flight, which usually takes place on a warm, sunny day, everything is sacrificed for lightness. Even most of the intestinal aids, the one-celled animals, are lost before the insects take to the air. With their bodies thin, the termites soar away on their rather weak wings, always flying in the direction the breeze is blowing.

Near the base of the wings of the termites there is a suture, or line of weakness. After the flight, the wings break off here, leaving the insects free for their underground existence. Sometimes, one of the wings will snap off in midair and the termite will drop to earth, spinning like a maple seed.

During these spreading flights, millions of the insects perish. Bears, rats, skunks, birds and lizards devour many of them. In Africa, natives sometimes surround a nest before the swarm, bringing broad leaves in which to collect the insects, which are greatly prized as table delicacies. Frequently, children in East Africa will make a rhythmical tapping with little sticks outside a nest, simulating rainfall to entice the insects out. Many of these tropical termites swarm only after rains.

Vibrations affect termites within their dark homes as sights and sounds do us. Most termites are completely blind. They "feel" their way through life aided by delicate "vibration preceptors" on their legs, antennae, and other parts of the body. Within the nest, they seem to communicate by a sort of wireless telegraphy of vibrations.

When disturbed, for example, workers and soldiers have been observed making rapid, convulsive movements in unison. They may be broadcasting an alarm by vibration-radio. Termite soldiers often strike their heads against wood and those of one species which inhabit the dry stalks of the Spanish bayonet flower in desert regions of the Southwest, produce a sound which can be heard several feet away in this manner. It is interesting to note that the thousands of miles of railroad ties laid down in the United States are rarely attacked by termites. The vibrations produced by passing trains seem to keep them away. Also, there is little danger of termites attacking the walls of a factory when vibrating machines are running.

After swarming, the termites land and pair off. Each pair begins digging, back to back, to start a new colony. About a week after the flight is over, and the underground chamber has been finished, the king and queen of the future colony mate. The largest colonies are found in the tropics where nests are often higher than a man's head. Some of these nests have occupied the same position for half a century or more. The most curious of the termite skyscraper homes is one found in Australia. It rises to a height of almost a dozen feet and has its broad sides always facing east and west. Almost with the accuracy of a compass needle, the narrow ends point north and south. Other termites, in the Belgian Congo, construct homes that rise above the ground like huge mushrooms. The conical roof acts like an umbrella, shedding the rain. Down the trunks of jungle trees in the rain-forests of British Guiana, still other termites construct long tunnels of earth-like particles cemented together, and along these runways they add finger-shaped projections slanting out from either side to form gutters and divert the water from the tunnel.

The huge nests of many tropical termites are carefully air-conditioned to keep the interiors at a uniform temperature. In Africa, a large reptile called the Nile Monitor breaks into termite nests and lays its eggs in the warm interior, leaving them there to hatch. Birds, resembling parrots, in South America, excavate nest holes in the sides of the arboreal nests of certain termites. They lay their eggs and raise their young there.

All told, scientists have described and named about 2,000 different kinds of termites. The country that has the greatest number of different kinds is Ethiopia.

In the United States, there are approximately forty species. Ninety-five per cent of the damage done by termites is produced by species which nest in the ground. These subterranean insects are rarely seen except during the swarming flight. The workers, which remain in the darkness of their tunnels throughout their lives, produce the most serious damage. Even when wooden structures have concrete foundations,— if they are too low—the termites bridge the gaps by constructing tunnels of dirt particles cemented together. Sometimes these tubes branch like the veins of a leaf. At other times, they hang like ropes or vines straight down through the air from the underside of a floor to the earth below.

In deserts, termites build such tubes far down into the ground to protect themselves in case the wind blows away the drifting top sand. As you follow along a narrow termite tunnel built on the side of a concrete foundation, you will sometimes see widened portions which act as "sidetracks." Here, insects traveling in opposite directions can pass each other.

In their lifelong search for cellulose, the termites produce damage in a wide variety of forms. Airplanes have been weakened while standing in hangars. Pipe organs have been riddled in churches. Stored rifles have had their stocks turned to "sawdust." And real sawdust has been attacked by the insects even when it was in an icehouse filled with ice! Books, bonds, Bibles and blueprints all have been damaged by the inroads of the termites.

Because they work under cover and are protected by tunnels and underground chambers, the insects are difficult to combat. The best summary of how to fight termites I have seen, is contained in the book, *Our Enemy, the Termite* by Thomas E. Snyder. Since 1909 the author of this book has been studying and experimenting with termites as a government entomologist. He tells one story that illustrates the difficulties besetting the path of the termite specialist.

In Panama, he noticed a curious cone-shaped nest in an isolated tree in a pasture. He was part way up the trunk when he encountered a vine with sharp thorns that pierced his skin. Next, he bumped into a wasp nest and the infuriated insects poured out and attacked him. He lost his hold and fell to the ground. Then, when he knocked the cone nest down with a stick and broke into it, he found, instead of the expected termites, a legion of vicious ants that bit him unmercifully. He was just shaking them free when he turned and saw a bull charging at him across the pasture. Once safe beyond the pasture fence, he called it a day and went home nursing his bites and scratches.

While such a chain of misfortunes is rare, the investigator who becomes interested in termites is likely to be in for difficulties under any conditions. The insects are difficult to watch; secretive in their habits. We still have much to learn about them. But what we do know makes them seem well worth additional watching.

Chapter XII

WALKING STICKS AND PRAYING MANTISES

Among the leaves of bushes and trees, you sometimes encounter strange, slim insects with ungainly legs and threadlike antennae. Their bodies are as long as your forefinger, yet hardly thicker than a match. These insects, which resemble slender twigs on legs, are known as walking sticks.

They are relatives of the grasshopper and the cricket, and are found all over the United States. None of the sixteen species natives to North America have wings although some of the tropical walking sticks can fly. You rarely see these insects unless they move. Their green and brown protective coloration and their twig-like form provide an almost perfect camouflage.

Some summers, however, these strange creatures appear in vast numbers, stripping the leaves from trees like a plague of locusts. Once, in Michigan, they infested an oak forest covering 2,500 acres. There were literally millions of the insects and the dropping of their eggs sounded like the patter of rain.

These eggs, like tiny brilliant-black seeds with a white stripe down one side, are hardly an eighth of an inch long. The female lets them fall to the ground instead of planting them carefully, as many other insects do. However, this is the best way of concealing them, for they are soon covered by drifting leaves and thus are hidden from the eyes of birds and mice. In the tropics, one kind of walking stick has a sort of gun at the tip of its tail by means of which it can shoot the eggs for considerable distances, thus scattering them and increasing their chances of being overlooked.

After lying on the ground from one to two years, the eggs hatch into fragile pale-green midgets with coal-black eyes. The hatching occurs soon after the juicy leaf buds are out. Only about two out of every hundred eggs, it is estimated, produces a young walking stick. But, the number of eggs laid is tremendous. On the floor of an infested forest, a few years ago, an investigator found an average of more than 50 eggs to a square foot of ground.

Walking on threadlike legs, the young insects seek out tender leaves. Eating from the edges, or biting holes in the leaves, they consume the tissue, leaving the framework of veins behind. Late at night, I have found these curious "twigs that walk" active on the leaves of low-lying bushes. Their favorite food appears to be the leaves of oak trees.

At first light green, the insects turn brownish later in the year when most of the twigs have lost their greenish hue. How such color change protects them from the birds which are ever on the watch is shown by a simple experiment. A scientist once tethered green and brown praying mantises, related to the walking

sticks, to leaves, putting 45 green ones on green leaves
and 65 brown ones on brown and withered leaves. At
the end of seventeen days' exposure to birds, all had
survived. Then he reversed the insects and put the
green ones on the brown leaves and the brown ones on
the green leaves. At the end of eleven days, all of the
green insects and 55 out of the 65 brown ones had
been discovered and eaten.

Some of the walking sticks, when you disturb them,
play possum. A naturalist once timed one of these
sham deaths and found the walking stick remained
rigid and unmoving for nearly *six hours!* A few of
these insects, like starfish and daddy longlegs, grow a
new leg if one is broken off.

In the Southeastern part of the United States you
find a walking stick which is known as the "musk
mare." It gives off an evil-smelling fluid which smarts
like fire if it gets in your eyes. The largest of our
American walking sticks lives in Louisiana and the
surrounding territory. It grows to be six inches long.
But it is only a "baby brother" to an East Indian relative. This largest insect alive sometimes reaches a
length of fifteen inches.

The Praying Mantis, the walking stick's relative, is
found in Southern and Eastern states. It is one of the
most unusual insects alive. As long as your hand and
green or brown, it waits for its prey motionless, with
spiked forelegs raised as though in an attitude of
prayer. This gives it its name. But it could be more
truly spelled Preying Mantis, for this bloodthirsty

creature preys on all kinds of insects from plant lice to butterflies. The fact that it eats a vast number of beetles, bugs and caterpillars makes it a valuable friend of the gardener and farmer.

I have seen one of these insects dining on a dragon-fly and once I saw a half-grown one stalking a black swallowtail far larger than itself. These insects will battle a kitten or a bird without showing fear. A few years ago, traffic in an Ohio city was tied up while motorists stopped to watch a sparrow and a mantis fighting in the middle of the street. Even after its head has been severed in battle, a mantis will still stand on its feet and raise its wings as though in conflict.

However, these fierce-natured creatures are not only harmless to man but they make most interesting pets. Every summer, I collect them in August and September. Oftentimes they stay on one bush or in one part of a garden for weeks so you are able to become acquainted with different individuals. You see them poised awaiting the approach of their prey, or stalking like cats over the leaves. When within reach, their forelegs shoot out and the toothed blades snap shut like the jaws of a steel trap, holding the prisoner beyond hope of escape. In the Orient, mantises are sometimes tethered to bedposts to catch flies and mos-quitoes.

During the winter, you can collect the egg cases which these insects leave attached to weeds and bushes. The cases are brownish and about the size of a walnut. From them, hatch 200 or more honey-yellow, dark-eyed baby insects. They all emerge from the front of the egg case and dangle from silken threads. Masses of the insects hang together like a bunch of tiny animated bananas. After all have broken free, the silk threads remain, forming a small tassel of white on the brown and empty ball.

Follow the young mantises through the grass and weeds and you will find them dining on little insects like plant lice. They are carnivorous from birth to death, always preferring living prey. But, in captivity, I have kept them alive by feeding them dead crickets and bits of hamburger and corned beef. They also need watering every day. The moisture can be placed like dew, sprinkled on the leaves around them, or you can hold a spoon with water in it to their mouths and after they become tame they will bend down and drink like a horse at a trough. The baby insects as they come from the egg case are hardly larger than mosquitoes. By the end of summer, many have grown until they are four inches long. The young mantises seem to disappear after they leave the egg case and then to reappear late in summer. The explanation is that they are so perfectly camouflaged that they are not seen until they are large and catch the eye.

In the fall, after the mantises have mated, the female engages in a mystifying cannibal feast, devouring her husband! One explanation for this puzzling occurrence is that, ages ago, the gruesome habit helped the mantis survive. As soon as the mating is over, the usefulness of the male is ended and if he is killed at once, the food he would consume afterwards is conserved for the females who will lay the eggs and insure the continuation of the species. There is no such thing as a "man's world" among the insects. Ants and bees and wasps, the most highly developed of the insects, all are ruled by queens. Among the six-legged, the males are usually smaller and play a minor role.

One of the last things the female mantis does before the cold of autumn ends her life is to make the curious ball of froth which forms the egg case. If you catch a dozen or so females in late September and place them on twigs in the house, the chances are that some will make their egg cases while you are watching. You will have plenty of time to see what is going on, for the process takes sometimes as long as three hours. I once watched a female work painstakingly and deliberately, consuming a full three hours in the building of a walnut-sized housing for her eggs.

Whitish froth squeezes from the tip of the insect's abdomen like toothpaste coming from a tube. By moving the tip of the abdomen about in gradually widening circles, as she hangs head downward, she attaches the material to a twig and builds up the case in the manner of a threshing machine building a straw-stack. In the center of this ball of froth, she deposits her cluster of eggs. After the job is completed, the insect walks away without even looking back at the house she has made to protect the eggs that will produce children she will never live to see.

About 1898, the European mantis was introduced

accidentally into New York State near Rochester, one or more of the egg-cases coming into the country attached to packing material around nursery stock. In a similar manner, a few years earlier, an Oriental mantis reached a nursery near Philadelphia, Pennsylvania. A quarter of a century later, another mantis from the Orient, an insect with narrower wings and the scientific name of *Tenodera angustipennis*, made its appearance in Maryland. These two Oriental insects can be told apart easily by colored spots between their forelegs. The spot is yellow on the original China mantis, orange on the narrower-winged species. A smaller native mantis, characterized by short wings that do not reach to the tip of its tail, is found throughout the southern part of the United States.

Because a hungry praying mantis consumes insect pests, gardeners in many parts of the country have been interested in putting the insect's appetite to work. One Midwestern nursery, for a number of years, sold the egg-cases of the China mantis for "planting" on bushes in gardens to increase the number of praying mantises in the area. Wherever a colony was established in this way, the insects spread out and populated the surrounding territory. Thus the China mantis spread rapidly westward through northern states. By 1952, it had reached the Pacific and was established in California.

Chapter XIII

WASPS

IF YOU were asked to pick the three smartest insects, which ones would you choose? Scientists say they are the ants, the bees and the wasps. All these members of the insect "brain trust" belong to the same order, the Hymenoptera (hi′-me-nop′-tera), or membrane-winged insects. Of the three, the wasps seem to be the cleverest and the quickest to learn by experience.

One summer, I spent hours watching the building of a nest by paper-making wasps. At first, all the workers made trips afield to find wood out of which they bit chunks and chewed them into pulp for making paper. Then, I noticed one of the wasps had discovered a short-cut. It had found a heavy cardboard tag dangling from a piece of string. Time after time, it visited the tag, gouging out pieces of the ready-made paper which it chewed up and added to the nest. When I took the tag away temporarily, it circled around the spot for a quarter of an hour at a time, alighting, darting this way and that, searching frantically for its lost "paper mine."

While these clever insects are adding to their nests, you will notice that they always work backwards so they do not walk on the moist, newly applied pulp-paper. From time to time, they test it with their feelers, apparently to determine if it is just the proper thickness. As the colony increases in size, some wasps add more stories to their paper homes. Skyscraper nests are made by one tropical wasp. They contain as many as forty layers of cells, one below the other.

Because the insects get their wood fibers from different sources, the color of the paper may vary in different parts of the nest. In some cases, where the insects have bitten pieces from the boards of a painted barn, lines of red have been found running across the gray material which composed the rest of the nest. One curious wasp of British Guiana builds a home of reddish-brown paper on the outside of which it places decorations in the form of stripes and masses of white, pink or green. When completed, the nest looks like a frosted cupcake.

Both the yellow jacket and the bald-faced hornet belong to the paper-making clan. So long as you do not meddle with their nests, they are peaceful creatures. But, if you are in search of trouble with a capital T, all you have to do is poke a hornet's nest. Some of these nests are as big as a half-bushel basket and contain thousands of inmates.

Other paper-making wasps build their nests in the earth, like bumblebees. But, one and all, their colonies have substantially the same life history. They begin with a single queen who has spent the winter in hibernation, safe in a cranny or buried in some heap of trash. She starts building the nest and as the six-sided cells are completed, she lays an egg in each. Pale, legless grubs hatch out and the queen becomes nurse as well as nest builder. Later, as the grubs turn into adults, they take up the work of helping their mother and enlarging the nest. Each adult, as it comes from its inverted cradle, crawls first of all, from grub to grub, tapping each on the head until it gives off a small drop of fluid which the newborn wasp licks up greedily. This is its first meal. Shortly afterwards, it is strong enough to begin foraging expeditions in search of food and wood fibers.

The adults live mostly on nectar, the grubs are the ones that demand meat. This is supplied in the form of "hamburgers." The full-grown wasps capture other insects and with their jaws bite them methodically until they are made into a mincemeat which the grubs can swallow. After a week or two of gathering wood, a wasp exhausts the saliva which it mixes with the fibers as it chews them. After that, the insect confines itself to hunting and caring for the young. So, when you see a wasp adding paper to a nest, you know it is one of the younger inhabitants of the insect city.

Toward the end of the summer season, larger cells are built in the nests to house the young queens. In fall, these queens, after mating, secrete themselves where they will be safe during the winter. All the rest of the colony, all of the thousands of insect papermakers which have inhabited the nest, die in the first cold snap. Even if they are brought indoors, fed and kept in a warm place, they grow sluggish and soon die, apparently of old age. The deserted nests are never used a second time.

This is the life story of the "social" wasps which construct nests and live together in colonies. Besides them, there are 10,000 different kinds of "solitary" wasps. They live a "lone wolf" existence, each female preparing an individual home which it stocks with food for its young. These wasps are the most interesting of all.

One is known as the "cicada killer." This black-and-yellow huntress transports to its underground burrow "dog-day harvest flies" larger than itself. Sometime, on a hot summer afternoon, you may be lucky enough to see an insect whirring down on a long slant to a bumpy landing. It is the cicada killer heading with a victim for its burrow. Time after time, it will toil up the trunk of a tree tugging at its burden. Then at the tip of a branch it will grip its captive with its legs and launch out in the direction of its burrow. The cicada is so heavy the wasp cannot support it in flight, but it is able to progress on a long slant, in the manner of a flying squirrel. One of these wasps will make as many as half a dozen glides in the course of its toilsome journey home. At its burrow, it pulls the cicadas it catches inside, lays an egg on one of them and then seals up the cavern. In the course of time, the egg will hatch and the wasp grub will feed on the paralyzed but still living cicadas with which the burrow is stocked. The following spring, it emerges a full-fledged cicada killer itself.

This is the life cycle of most of the other solitary wasps. Many of them have only a single kind of prey. One hunts aphides almost exclusively, another crab spiders, another a certain kind of caterpillar. In each case, they sting the victim with almost uncanny skill, injecting a fluid which paralyzes the nerves but does not produce death. Thus, the grubs will find fresh food when they break from the egg.

In getting this food to the burrows, the wasps overcome many obstacles and in doing so earn their place in the insect "brain trust." Here are a few instances showing how they use ingenuity and foresight:

Ammophila, a sand wasp, often brings home caterpillars three or four times her weight. In dragging them, she always turns them over on their backs so they slide along like the runners on a sled. Once, Phil Rau tells us, he saw one of these wasps near St. Louis, Mo., having difficulty getting a caterpillar through a tangle of grass. It solved the problem by moving forward first one end and then the other, just as a lone workman would advance a heavy timber. Wasps have spent as long as two hours dragging caterpillars 100 yards through thick grass to reach their burrows.

Another wasp which specializes in hunting spiders, always makes it a habit to hang its victim up in the crotch of a weed or grass stalk while it is digging the burrow. This keeps ants from disturbing its prey while the wasp is busy.

Even more astonishing is the action of another spider-hunter which makes its burrow near the water. It will transport heavy burdens across a pond or stream by dragging the spiders through the water, towing them behind while pulling with buzzing wings. As the wasp heads for its burrow, the trailing spider leaves a wake like that behind a speeding motorboat.

In preparing their burrows, different solitary wasps use different methods. The great steel-blue diggers will send out a steady stream of dirt and sand as they work. I once saw two of these wasps tear into hard-packed cinders without any apparent difficulty. Most wasps use their legs to hurl back the material they excavate. Sometimes they send it several inches from the mouth of the burrow. A few wasps bite out chunks and one brings water and moistens the ground so it can ball up little pellets of earth and carry out the material in this manner. One of the tiniest of all wasps, called the Diodontus americanus, carries the sand grains out in its jaws and with its legs. It takes this midget an hour or more to construct a tiny burrow where it stores the plant lice on which it preys. Before it seals up the opening, this wasp places from five to forty aphides inside to provide food for the young wasp which will hatch from the egg. In the underground nest of another wasp, you will find flies laid one on top of the other like cordwood, the heads all pointing in the same direction!

Usually, a solitary wasp digs its burrow, then closes the entrance and hunts the prey to stock the cavern be-

fore it opens it again. If it places several insects in the
burrow, it will carefully close up the entrance each
time it sets out in search of new victims. Some digger
wasps pound down the dirt, using stones or sticks or the
legs of insects to tamp the earth smooth, holding these
hammers in their jaws. You will see the insects almost
standing on their heads during this part of the work.
In fact, one wasp does stand on its head and pounds
down the dirt like a pile driver, using its flat "face"
for a hammer!

When the insects have finished smoothing and
tamping the dirt, there is nothing left to show the location of the underground burrow. Yet, one of the
Bembix sand wasps returns to its burrow-site flying
high in the air and drops straight down, landing exactly at the point where it is necessary for it to dig to
gain entrance to its cave. When it leaves, it does the
same thing in reverse, rising until it is almost out of
sight. In their fascinating book, *Wasp Studies Afield*,
Phil and Nellie Rau tell of seeing one of these insects
capture a bug on a cocklebur bush, only ten feet from
the burrow-site. Instead of flying directly home, it
darted high into the air, flew over the ten feet and
came down almost as straight as an elevator to land
with its burden at the door of its burrow!

How do the wasps know the location of their little
caves? The homing instinct of these insects has been
a puzzle for years. Evidence points to the conclusion
that they follow landmarks just as we do. The Raus
tell of a mud wasp that always flew to a railroad track,

parallel to it until it came to a pond, and then home, rather than heading straight for its objective.

Once, when a little piece of white paper was pinned to the ground to help the Raus find the entrance of a burrow, the female wasp used it as a guide. When the paper was removed, she had a great deal of trouble finding her burrow. On another occasion, a two-foot bush near a nest was cut off and stuck in the ground three or four feet away. The wasp became confused. It flew to the bush a dozen times proving that it had used the object as a landmark in finding its burrow.

Oftentimes, you will see a solitary wasp walk around and around the closed burrow before it takes off on its hunting flight. It will hop into the air and fly in widening circles until finally it darts off across the fields. The action suggests a man looking back at every turn in a strange town so he will be able to find his way home again.

The biggest and most fearsome of the digger wasps is the steel-blue Tarantula Hawk of the Southwest. Its prey are the great hairy tarantula spiders which it attacks like a bolt of lightning and paralyzes with a single jab of its stinger.

An entirely different kind of solitary wasp is the mud user. Everyone is familiar with the cartridge-like cells of the common mud-dauber. They are often attached to the walls of garages and barns but they may be found in a wide variety of curious places. They are sometimes made in the tubes of corn-planting machines stored in barns. Once, a flag was unfurled for the Fourth of July and a wasp nest fell out. It had been made inside the folds of the cloth. Even more curious is a story reported from Oklahoma. A man repaired his automobile engine in the backyard. The job took him several days. Afterwards, he couldn't make his car run more than twenty miles an hour. At a garage, the timing, the carburetor, the fuel lines were all tested. Each was in good condition. Finally, the engine was torn down in search of the trouble. In the manifold port on the side of the motor, a mud-dauber had built its nest when the engine was being overhauled in the owner's backyard. When this mud nest was removed, the motor functioned perfectly.

By any puddle of water, on a hot summer day, you will find these mason wasps busy collecting the little balls of mud with which they fashion their cells. After they have filled them with paralyzed spiders and insects, they lay their eggs and seal up the chambers. You can have fun watching these wasps at work by making an artificial mudpuddle in a corner of your backyard or even in an old tin pan.

Not only are wasps the first paper-makers and masons, but they also are the first jug makers. One little member of the Hymenoptera tribe fashions minute jug-shaped chambers of mud. I have found them attached oftenest to goldenrod. Within these adobe shells, the young wasps live through the winter, to emerge as adults the following spring. Among the solitary wasps, only the immature survive the cold. All the adults are killed.

If you watch wasps at work, you will soon see them demonstrating their ability to learn from experience. One experimenter tells of taking a caterpillar away from a wasp and placing it in a glass vial. The wasp returned, walked around on the vial, seeing her prey but unable to reach it. It never occurred to her to enter the open neck of the bottle. When the experimenter put the caterpillar at the open end, the wasp seized it almost at once. Again the caterpillar was taken away and this time placed in the middle of the vial. The wasp quickly entered the open end and dragged out her prey. She had learned in one lesson how to overcome an unusual situation.

While the wasps oftentimes surprise us with their seeming intelligence, at other times they reveal how much they are run by instinct. One of the strangest of these examples comes from a laboratory where a scientist imprisoned a worker wasp in a container holding a grub of its own species. The wasp knew it must feed the grub, in its prison, but it was unable to find anything to do it with. Finally, in desperation, it bit off the grub's rear end and tried to feed it to the front end!

Chapter XIV

COLLECTING WITH A CAMERA

WHEN you collect insects with a camera as well as with a net, the thrills of home exploring are doubled. And the sport of insect photography has a double thrill in itself. Stalking your game and snapping the picture are fun enough. But you have added excitement of seeing your photograph develop into a permanent record of the insect—just as it looked in natural surroundings and everyday action. A series of such pictures adds greatly to the interest of your collected specimens.

The bigger the insect, the easier it is to photograph. Even if you have nothing more than a cheap box-camera, you can snap the pictures of the larger six-legged creatures—the butterflies, moths and dragonflies. By using a portrait attachment on such a camera, you can get closer to your subject and can record it larger on your film.

One way of getting your insect subjects at close range is to notice the particular plants upon which they alight. Butterflies of different species often show preference for special flowers and dragonflies will alight again and again on the same cattails and rushes. Pick out, for example, some prominent milkweed plant in full bloom. Station yourself with your camera focused on the flowers. You can measure the distance from camera to flower beforehand to be sure of the focus. Then, wait until one of the Monarch butterflies, which flock to milkweeds to sip their favorite nectar, alights. As it hangs motionless, snap your shutter. It is best to use fast shutter speed as few people can hold a camera perfectly still for more than 1-25th second. If you move the camera, the image on the film will be blurred.

Until you can estimate distances accurately, always measure off the number of feet from your position to the plant on which you are focusing and set the camera accordingly. When you have developed skill at judging distances, you can begin stalking the insects. After you have set your camera so it will be in focus at a certain distance, approach slowly until you are within "shooting range" of some insect on a plant. Then snap the shutter. In such work, disregard the old maxim for amateur snap-shooting: "Keep the sun at your back." Rather, be sure the sun is overhead or from one side. If it is from your back, it is likely to cast your shadow ahead, spoiling your picture or frightening away your quarry.

As soon as you begin taking up insect photography in earnest, it will pay you to buy a pocket notebook and record a few facts about every picture you snap. Put down the subject, the place, the time of day, the lighting conditions, the kind of film used, the lens opening and the shutter speed. Later on, by comparing this information with the developed films, you can learn what you did wrong and how to remedy your mistakes. Another aid to better pictures is a reliable exposure meter, giving you the correct exposure needed for each individual shot. Nothing is more discouraging than finding a picture which was snapped at the end of half an hour's stalking, spoiled because you gave the wrong exposure.

Although a box camera or simple folding outfit will enable you to start recording the pictures of the larger insects, the vast tribes of smaller creatures, which make up the bulk of the insect population, will be beyond reach of your hunting equipment. You will need a better camera for the work. The two most important features are: 1. A ground-glass back, or focusing mechanism, which will enable you to get your subject in perfect focus. 2. A long-extension bellows, permitting you to get close to a small insect and thus record a larger image on the film. If the closest you can get is several feet, the insect is likely to look like a fly-speck on the developed negative.

Most of the thousands of insect pictures I have taken have been made with the same $3\frac{1}{4}''$ x $4\frac{1}{4}''$ Ideal B, Zeiss camera. I bought it secondhand and have used it for almost ten years. It has traveled more than 15,000 miles and has recorded pictures all the way from the Everglades of Florida to the North Woods of Maine. I will long remember the thrill of seeing the sharp, detailed image of a Monarch butterfly appear on a negative in the darkroom—the first picture taken with this camera. All the photographs in this book were made with the same sturdy outfit.

Whatever kind of a camera you use, it will pay to put it on a tripod or other solid support as often as possible. This holds the camera perfectly steady and also keeps it in one position after it has been focused. Also, it permits longer exposures which are sometimes necessary to record detail. The farther you "stop down" the diaphragm opening on the camera, the greater will be your "depth of focus," or the distance from the nearest to the farthest object in the picture that is perfectly clear and sharp. Because, in photographing insects, you are working so close to your subject, the depth of focus is extremely shallow. So, whenever possible, stop down to f 22 or below. It will give you clearer, sharper pictures.

However, the farther you stop down, the longer you have to leave the shutter open. At f 22, for example, the exposure required is four times as long as at f 11. So, you have to experiment to find out how long you can give the exposure without having the insect move. Even the slightest movement, under such conditions, will mean a blurred picture. Using fast, supersensitive film is a help.

Various tricks have been tried for making insects hold still long enough to photograph them. If they can't fly away, you can sometimes tire them out by putting them in a desired position over and over again until they remain quiet. Some insect photographers give subjects a sniff of ammonia or ether and then place them where they want them, snapping their pictures when they revive. In this way, pictures can be planned out in advance. However, be sure the plant you use for the resting place of your subject is one on which the insect is likely to be found in nature. A Cecropia moth on a lily, for example, would be of little value, for the simple reason that these moths never visit flowers, for they never eat.

Incidentally, never use dead insects for your pictures. Such fakes can be detected easily. If you use dead butterflies or moths for practice shots at the start, be sure to mark such negatives so they won't get mixed up with the real pictures you make later on.

Most insects are less active when they are cold. So, sometimes you can place a butterfly or other subject in an icebox until it is chilled into relative inactivity and then put it in the spot where the camera is focused. Also, the fact that moths fly at night and butterflies in the daytime can be used to advantage. You can photograph moths during daylight when they are naturally at rest and you can snap butterflies after dark when they are sleepy.

For this and other night work, you will need photoflood bulbs. A pair of gooseneck lamps will concentrate the light and can be adjusted in any desired position.

When you are taking the pictures of insects with gauzy wings, such as damsel-flies or lacewings, having the sun or the photoflood light coming at an angle from the rear—being careful not to let it shine directly into the lens—will produce striking "backlighting" effects. Slightly longer exposures will be required to bring out the detail with such lighting. The three diagrams, in Fig. 17, show three types of lighting for insect photography.

If you want to "bring the outdoors indoors," and still get natural pictures of insects, one method is to use glass cages. Through these transparent houses, you can focus your camera and then snap the shutter when

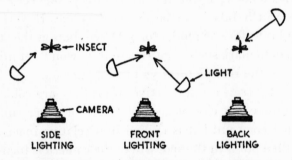

Fig. 17.—Three Types of Lighting for Photographing Insects.

the insects, placed on natural plant surroundings within, assume interesting positions. For small bugs, you can make little cages out of the thin, clear lantern-slide-cover glasses which can be purchased for a few cents at any photographic supply house. For larger cages, use glass walls that are clear and free from defects. Plate glass, being perfectly smooth, is best for this purpose. However, it is more expensive than ordinary window glass. Be careful in photographing the occupants of these insect "glass houses" that the light is coming from an angle which will throw no glare or reflection from the glass into the lens.

Oftentimes, without using a "glass house," you can make tabletop insect pictures by placing a subject that is not too lively on flowers or weeds before a white sheet of cardboard. Adjusting your lights so they do not throw shadows on the background, focus the camera to take in the part of the plant on which the insect is resting naturally. You can take such pictures when rain or wind makes outdoor shooting impossible.

To get really good pictures of very small creatures, you must have patience as well as film. Lee Passmore, the noted photographer of spiders, worked for 300 nights near his home in southern California before he obtained his famous series of photographs showing the life of the trap-door spider. Most of the work was done with photoflash lamps, the camera being focused on a burrow and the flashlight being set off when the spider appeared.

A series of pictures, showing succeeding steps in an action or the life history of an insect, always has added interest. When exploring with your camera be on the alert for opportunities to capture on film such events as an insect shedding its skin, a great moth coming from its cocoon and unfolding its wings, a larva turning into its chrysalis or spinning its cocoon.

In conclusion, here are a dozen suggestions for getting better insect pictures. In the beginning, you will be interested in only part of them. But if you continue collecting with a camera as well as with a net, you will find all of them of assistance.

1. Don't guess at distances. If you use a box camera or folding outfit, measure the number of feet from camera to subject each time until you have developed skill at estimating distances accurately.

2. Put down the facts about each picture, as you make it, for later reference.

3. Get in the habit of using a tripod instead of taking just snapshots with the camera held in your hand.

4. Stop down your camera whenever possible instead of taking the pictures with the lens wide open.

5. Use fast film. Supersensitive film permits you to stop down farther and still use the same speed.

6. Panchromatic film, sensitive to all colors, including red, is best for insect work. If you use "color blind," or ordinary film, a red-and-black bug photographs all black.

7. Don't guess at exposures. As soon as you can afford it, buy an exposure meter. It will pay for itself in the long run by reducing spoiled film.

8. If in doubt about an exposure for an important picture, take three shots, one exposed at the time you think is right, a second at twice that time and a third at half that time. With the latitude of modern films, one of those shots should give you a satisfactory negative.

9. Whenever possible, take a series of pictures that shows related actions, or the life story of an insect, rather than isolated photos.

10. Develop, or have your films developed, in fine-grain developer. Oftentimes, you will find you will want to enlarge a small section of a negative and unless you use fine-grain developer, the enlargement will be marred by the graininess of the picture.

11. Keep your good negatives in envelopes or manila "preservers." If you dump them all loosely together, they will become scratched and spoiled.

12. Finally, always strive to record story-telling pictures rather than mere "catalogue" photographs. A picture that shows an insect doing something unusual and interesting is worth many shots of the same insect doing nothing or in uninteresting surroundings. Try to get pictures that show clearly every tiniest detail, and at the same time form striking photographs which will catch the eye.

Chapter XV

DRAGONFLIES

IF YOU lived under the water like a fish when you were a baby and up in the air like a bird when you were an adult; if you could eat your weight in beefsteaks in half an hour; if you could keep right on climbing up a ladder after your head had been cut off, your life would be as strange as that of the dragonfly.

This familiar insect lives underwater as a nymph, sometimes for years, before it develops wings and takes to the air. It has been known to devour more than its weight in horseflies in half an hour. One dragonfly was captured with so many mosquitoes in its mouth it couldn't close it. The tightly packed mass contained more than 100 of these insect pests. And, several times, these graceful fliers have been seen, when their heads were accidentally severed from their bodies, to continue climbing up a reed or stick!

The ignorant and superstitious believe that dragonflies bring water snakes to life, kill livestock and sew up the ears of wading boys. They are called snake-feeders and snake-doctors, devil's-darning-needles and mule-killers. As a matter of fact, they have no stingers to sting with, no needles to use in sewing, and they are no more a friend of snakes than we are. By catching mosquitoes and flies, they rid the world of many pests.

So, the next time a mosquito starts his little dentist's drill and begins boring through your skin, think kindly of your friend, the dragonfly!

There are about 2,500 different kinds of these hawk-like insects. Three hundred kinds are found in the United States. The name of their order: Odonata (O'-do-na'-ta) means "toothed" and refers to the needle-sharp teeth in the mouth of the insects. In addition to dragonflies, there are about seventy-five kinds of damsel-flies in the United States. These are smaller and frailer members of the Odonata clan. You can distinguish damsel-flies from dragonflies in several ways. They flutter from one perch to another and never hawk about with the swift bold flight of the dragonflies. When at rest, the dragonflies hold their wings out straight while the damsel-flies usually fold theirs vertically over their bodies in the manner of butterflies. The forewings and hind-wings are similar in the dragonflies, dissimilar in the damsel-flies. In other respects, the life of the damsel-fly is similar to that of the larger dragonfly.

The first chapter in the life story of these familiar insects is the depositing of the eggs by the females. This is done in two ways. One is by bumping along the surface of a pond, dropping clumps of eggs into the water each time the tip of the abdomen touches the surface. The clumps are surrounded with a sort of gelatine which soon dissolves and lets the eggs fall to the bottom where they rest in the mud. Strangely enough, numerous tests have shown that the eggs will hatch only in dirty water. If you put some of these eggs in a glass of perfectly clean water, they will spoil, become moldy and never hatch. As many as 90,000 eggs have been found in a single clump deposited by a female dragonfly.

Different kinds of dragonflies choose different places in which to deposit their eggs. Some select still ponds, others rippling streams. Most of them leave their eggs in the water by flying low and dipping the tip of the abdomen as we have described. But some employ an even more spectacular method. They crawl down on the stem of a plant under the water and deposit their eggs in the fibers by cutting slits into which they press tiny white eggs, resembling rice kernels. When you see one of these females descending under the water, she seems to be silver-plated. A glistening film of air surrounds her. This supplies the needed oxygen while she is engaged in her egg-laying beneath the surface. If you encounter a female at work, wait until she flies away and then break off the plant and take it home. Place it in a jar of pond water and the eggs will hatch out into tiny nymphs.

Usually, the time required for hatching is from two to three weeks but in some species it is as short as five days. The creature which comes from the egg is as unlike the adult dragonfly as day is unlike night. It is a hideous little underwater ogre which skulks about the mud-bottom in search of living prey. It obtains oxygen through gills located at the lower end of the food canal. Its curious method of propelling itself, when it is alarmed, is to shoot the water backward from these gills, thus driving its body ahead like a rocket. I have seen nymphs only an inch long, drive themselves forward in a spurt of more than a foot in this manner. When they are being lifted out of an aquarium, the alarmed nymphs will often squirt water several feet away. Sometimes, nymphs I have collected have "played possum," feigning death. Then when they felt themselves safe in water they shot off like little rockets.

Another strange feature of their bodies, which will surprise you when you first see it in action, is a long underlip that folds back between their front legs. When the nymph nears its prey, this lower lip shoots out like a hand. Two claws at the end form a pair of pincers which grasp the victim. It is as though the nymph had an arm attached to its mouth. No other animal in the world has this aid to catching prey. The mask formed by this folding lip sometimes covers all the face of the nymph except its eyes. The movement of this appendage is as swift as the pounce of a cat. I have seen the lower lip flash in and out like a chameleon's tongue when the nymph was snapping up mosquito "wigglers" in an aquarium. In ten minutes, a ravenous nymph will devour as many as sixty larvae.

A nymph is entirely carnivorous. It will eat smaller water insects, tiny fish, and even other members of the dragonfly clan. If you put large and small nymphs in the same containers, you will see the big ones stalk and devour their smaller brothers. However, under natural conditions, the biggest nymphs fall prey themselves to other hunters. Crayfish eat many. Trout and other gamefish eat both nymphs and adult dragonflies. The stomach of one two-pound trout was found to contain the heads of thirty-five dragonflies. The hard head material was the last part of the bodies to be digested.

Damsel-fly nymphs develop rapidly. There may be several generations of these frail fliers in one season. The dragonflies are slower in reaching maturity, usually taking a full year, sometimes three and in some species even five years to attain full growth. Nymphs grow by shedding their skins, just as grasshoppers do. They may molt from eleven to fifteen times before they are full grown. Each time they shed their skin, the number of facets or lenses in the eyes increases. Some adult dragonflies have compound eyes with as many as 30,000 separate lenses in them. No other insect has keener eyesight than these swift aerial hunters. Some can detect movements fifty feet away. By having its head mounted on a sort of ball-and-socket joint, the dragonfly is able to look down and up as well as to either side.

Underwater, some nymphs have the power of altering the color of their bodies slightly to match their surroundings. Thus they are more effectively camouflaged and less likely to be observed by their enemies. Another amazing thing about these insect "water babies" is the way in which some of them can resist prolonged drought. The great Australian authority on dragonflies, R. J. Tillyard, tells of keeping nymphs in dry sand for three months. When he placed them in water at the end of that period they looked dried up and were so light they floated. Yet, they soon revived and began burrowing in the mud in their usual manner!

As the end of their water life approaches, the nymphs grow darker and their wing cases are more pronounced. They spend more and more time near the edge of the pond or stream in which they live, crawling about among the reeds and rushes. If you want to see the unforgettable sight of a dragonfly blossoming from the skin of an ugly nymph, tramp along the edge of a pond at dawn. Most of the species make their transformation early in the morning, usually before six o'clock. A few habitually come out about midnight. Numbers will sometimes make their transformation just before a thunderstorm, something in the climatic condition seeming to aid in the great adventure of entering the aerial world. Tillyard tells of seeing a large number of dragonflies emerge just as a storm was breaking. In ten minutes, they were out of their skins, their wings were expanded and they were soaring away to the protection of a near-by forest.

Usually, the transformation takes much longer than this. The nymph crawls up to some solid support, such as the stem of a water plant, a twig or a tree trunk. Here, it anchors itself and then begins straining until the skin on its back splits in a vertical rent. Little by little, it pulls its soft body from the old shell. The wings expand and harden, the new shell of skin solidifies like a suit of armor, and it darts away into the sunshine, riding through the air on swift wings after its long imprisonment under the water. Some dragonflies have their wings divided by veins into as many as 3,000 separate cells.

How swift those wings are has been the subject of much discussion. Accurate tests have shown that these insects, hardly longer than your finger, can equal the speed of an express train. One was timed traveling sixty miles an hour! Dragonflies are the most perfect airmen in the world. They can start, stop, hover and turn square corners. The Green Darner, probably the commonest dragonfly in all parts of the country, is full of curiosity. You will see it hover in front of you for half a minute at a time, coming back again and again to see what you are doing. I have had them perch on the end of my fishing rod with wings aquiver.

Large dragonflies often hunt over weedlots and meadows four or five miles away from the nearest water. They are strong fliers and when swamps dry up, great clouds of the insects migrate long distances in search of new hunting grounds. In the South Pacific, dragonflies have been known to migrate across a 200-mile strait from the Australian mainland to the Tasmanian coast.

Few of the world's creatures are more completely aerial than the dragonfly. Its legs are bunched so far

forward they are unfitted for walking. A dragonfly
clings and climbs but it never walks. The legs, however, have another purpose. As you will find if you
look at them closely, they are "feathered" with spines
that stick out either side. When the dragonfly is hunting on the wing, these spined legs form a basket·which
it uses to scoop up its prey while it is darting at top
speed through the air. The next time you are fishing,
watch one of these "darning needles" in action. A fly
buzzes near you. The "darning needle" shoots past and
the fly is gone. Such prey is eaten on the wing, in most
cases, with the inedible parts dropped to earth. Large
dragonflies will scoop up butterflies and in some instances have been seen to capture others of their own
kind on the wing. With quick bites of their jaws, they
will cut away the wings of the smaller dragonfly, and
then begin devouring the body in an aerial cannibal
feast.

Many kinds of dragonflies hawk back and forth
over regular beats. And woe to any other hunter that
poaches on their preserves. They dart at the intruder
and with a great rattle of wings he is driven off. But,
while the dragonflies are hunting their living prey,
other hunters are pursuing them. Birds snap them up;
spiders' webs entangle them; frogs leap into the air
and trout break the surface to capture low-flying skimmers. In the Malay Peninsula, natives smear long
sticks with birdlime and engage in the sport of catching dragonflies in the air. In old Japan, children used
to tie two beads or pebbles to the ends of a long hair.

They would toss this high in the air and dragonflies, pouncing on it under the impression it was a fly or other insect, would become entangled in the hair and the weight of the pebbles would bring the insect to earth.

The markings on dragonflies make them among the most beautiful creatures on earth. Some are emerald green, others copper, blue, violet, purple, bright red, orange, lemon yellow, French gray, pea green. Next to the butterflies and moths, a number of dragonflies will provide the most attractive part of your insect collection. They range from the frail and tiny damselfly relatives to the biggest dragonflies, with a wingspread of nearly seven inches. If you had been collecting millions of years ago in the great lush forests of the carboniferous era, you would have been able to catch dragonflies the size of hawks. Remains have shown that they had a wingspread of approximately thirty inches. These ancient ancestors of present-day dragonflies were the biggest insects that ever lived on earth.

Chapter XVI

WATER INSECTS

ON THE edge of a beaver bog, far back in the woods of Maine, I once spent the best part of a moonlight night crouching in a spruce blind, shooting flashlight pictures of beavers at work on their dam. A sharp rock was my only resting place in the blind. Hungry mosquitoes swarmed over my face and arms. By watching the gyrations of whirligig beetles, spinning on the brown surface of the water in the dusk, I was able to hold on until the beavers came. Spreading away in front of each bobbing nose, as the animals swam leisurely toward their dam, I could see a semicircle of darting water insects.

Everywhere, from the North Woods to southern lagoons, the calm waters of ponds and lazy streams are populated with aquatic insects. Every boy who has gone fishing, is acquainted with the surface skimmers —the water striders, the whirligig beetles and the water boatmen.

The most easily recognized are the whirligigs, dark, shiny little creatures that spin in circles on the surface of ponds and quiet coves. If you hold these insects in your hand for a time they will exude a milky white fluid which has a faint odor sometimes suggesting apples. Hence, in the Southwest, the beetles are called "apple bugs." Elsewhere they have local names such as "Vanilla bugs" and "dishwashers." Another interesting fact about these common creatures is this: their eyes are divided so half of each eye looks down into the water while the other half looks up into the air. Their rear legs are broadened into oars with which they scull rapidly through the water.

Female whirligigs lay white, cylindrical eggs, placing them end to end, in parallel rows on the leaves of water plants. Out of these eggs hatch slender creatures that suggest minute white centipedes. What appear to be legs on the rear half of their bodies are really feathery gills extending out on either side. These curious larvae creep over the decaying vegetation on the pond bottom, seeking young mayflies and other larvae which make up their food. When full-grown, they crawl out on the bank, their gills shrivel up and they prepare tiny cocoons, out of which they appear, weeks later, as full-fledged beetles. During winter, the whirligigs hibernate in the mud, reappearing again with the first fine days of spring.

Water-striders, or pond-skaters, are the slim, long-legged insects whose feet make dimples in the surface film. They also hibernate over winter. I have seen them darting about with their sudden spurts of speed, during February thaws. In sunshine, the dimples their feet produce cast splotches of light on the sand of shallow streams. Oftentimes, these spots catch your eye

before you see the grayish insect itself. If you watch
the legs of the strider closely, you will discover that
each of the three pairs has its own work to do. The
front pair is held out, ready to grasp food; the middle
pair propels the insect across the water, while the hind
pair does the steering.

Once I counted twenty-eight of these streamlined
water insects, all heading into a tiny waterfall above
a quiet pool in a mountain stream. Rhythmic kicks of
the middle legs kept them in position like a squadron
of destroyers.

Like the whirligig beetles, many water-striders have
wings. If their pools dry up, they fly away to other
ponds or streams. The eggs of the water-striders frequently are fastened to floating grass with waterproof
glue. In about two weeks, the young insects appear.
They are tiny creatures that closely resemble their
parents. During the following month, they shed their
skins five times as they grow to adult size. A thick,
velvetlike coating of hairs, covering the bodies of the
striders, holds air and thus supplies the creatures with
oxygen when they make their infrequent dives beneath the surface.

Another water insect with interesting habits is the
back-swimmer. This little creature has a back shaped
like the bottom of a canoe. When quiet, it hangs head
downward in the water, but when it is alarmed, it
swims rapidly away resting on its back and propelling
itself by two long, oar-like hind legs. These legs are
flattened and have a fringe of hairs which spread apart

on the pushing stroke and close up on the return
stroke, much in the manner of the webbed foot of a
duck. In case you try to handle a back-swimmer, be
prepared for a shock. These creatures can deliver a
stinging bite with their sharp little beaks.

Often confused with the back-swimmer is another
water insect, the water-boatman. It is similar in shape
and also uses its two long hind legs as oars. However,
it is smaller and never swims on its back. The males
have the curious habit of rubbing their forelegs on
their faces to produce a squeaking sound. The females
frequently glue their eggs to the backs of crayfish
where they remain until they hatch!

The female of another water insect, the giant water
bug, fastens her eggs with waterproof glue to the back
of the male. He carries 100 or more eggs, covering his
whole back, for ten days or so until the baby insects
appear.

Two other of the largest water insects are the Dytiscus and the Hydrophilus beetles. Both reach a length
of an inch and a half when full-grown. The larvae of
the Dytiscus are ferocious underwater dragons. They
sometimes attain a length of three inches and are
known as "water tigers." They attack and drain away
the lifeblood of tadpoles, other insect larvae, and even
small fish. Usually in shallows where tadpoles are
sunning themselves, you will find these insect tigers at
work. The adult Dytiscus beetles are almost as ravenous as the larvae. In a single afternoon, one of these
creatures confined in an aquarium devoured half a

dozen snails. One scientist kept a Dytiscus alive for three and a half years by feeding it bits of raw meat.

The Hydrophilus, or water scavenger beetle, feeds on decaying vegetation as well as living insects. I used to drop houseflies into the water of an aquarium in which one lived. It would cut off sections of the fly as neatly as though the job were done with a razor. Once, it devoured almost all of a large praying mantis. It returned to the dead floating insect, day after day.

Like the water tiger larvae of the Dytiscus, the young of the Hydrophilus prey upon tadpoles and underwater insects. The larvae of one kind of scavenger beetle is so hard to kill that it will live for an hour and a half in 95 per cent alcohol.

Many insects which spend their early lives in the water, fly away as soon as they become adults. Among these are the pestiferous midges, punkies, black flies and mosquitoes. Even these pests, however, have interesting histories. The black flies, for instance, before they emerge, ride to the surface of the water in bubbles of air. When the little humpbacked fly has completed its transformation within the pupa, the shell of the latter splits and the air-bubble, with the fly inside, rises to the surface, bursts and liberates the insect into its new home above the water.

In connection with mosquitoes: When one bites you, can you tell whether it is a male or female? The answer is simple. It is always a female. The males live on the juices of fruit and plants and never suck blood.

A common insect often mistaken for a large and

ferocious mosquito but which is, in reality, a harmless creature which cannot bite at all, is the crane fly. This insect is the daddy longlegs of the air. Its gangling, awkward, threadlike legs trail behind it when it flies. In the sandhill country of northern Indiana, we used to call crane flies "gallinippers" and thought they were giants of the mosquito tribe.

In spring and autumn, crane flies gather in swarms and dance in the air a few feet above the ground or water. Often at twilight, near some quiet marsh pond or stream, you will see them by the hundred bobbing up and down. On windy days, I have found scores clinging to the sheltered sides of apple trees, their long legs stretched out in front of them and anchored to the rough bark. In the manner of water-striders, they sometimes stand on the surface film of smooth water without breaking through. After drifting about, and apparently getting cool, they take off like an airplane on pontoons.

Another interesting insect which spends its early life in the water is the Dobson fly. Although it possesses strong pincerlike jaws it is said to eat nothing and to live but a short time in its adult form. The underwater larvae of the Dobson flies are the familiar bass bait, hellgrammites.

Caddis fly larvae are also widely known. Their fame comes from the houses they build. Out of bits of leaves, grains of sand, pebbles, pieces of twigs, and even tiny snailshells, these wormlike creatures construct cases in which they live with only their heads and front legs sticking out. Watch in some shallow pool on a summer day, and you are likely to see what appears to be a small stick, two or three inches long, suddenly begin to move along the bottom or up the stem of a water plant. The "stick" is the caddis worm's case to which it clings by means of stout hooks, facing forward at its tail. The case is lined with silk which the larva spins.

As these curious creatures grow, they add other and larger sections to the front of their house. Thus such cases often taper from front to rear. One species of caddis worm makes a "log cabin" out of bits of twig. Another kind is in the habit of using snailshells, often with the live snails inside, to decorate the outside of its home.

Some caddis worms construct what might be called fishing nets. These larvae spin little cup-shaped seines facing upstream. Then they take their places beside the nets and wait until the current brings food in the form of minute living creatures. Long before man first threw a net into the sea, these insects were waiting beside their seines and reaching in to get the food that caught in the webs! Caddis worms that spin nets are carnivorous. Other species live on vegetable matter. During the final stages of transformation, the caddis worm comes to the top of the water and changes into the brownish mothlike adult.

Of all the creatures you encounter among the water insects none has a stranger story than the frail-winged, short-lived mayfly. As a minute, burrowing under-

water larva, it spends as much as three years in the
mud and water below the surface. Then it becomes an
adult, leaves its discarded skin floating on the surface,
dances in the air, mates, and dies—all, oftentimes,
within a single day. During its adult life, it never
touches food. For so many generations has this been
going on that the mayfly has lost most of its mouth-
parts. Now, it couldn't eat if it wanted to. Another
curious fact about this creature is it is the only insect
in the world that has a second molt after it reaches full
size. It leaves the water encased in a sort of membrane
envelope which it discards before its mating flight.

Fish enjoy a banquet when these ephemeral creatures appear in vast clouds in the early spring. At such
times, trout fishermen reel in their lines and go home.
The competition is too great. Oftentimes, the hordes
of emerging mayflies reach fantastic numbers. At one
amusement park on the Great Lakes, carts had to be
hired to haul away the dead insects which piled up
under the electric lights. Some years ago, near Niagara
Falls, dead mayflies formed windrows a foot deep
under the street lamps of a neighboring town and fluttering clouds of the frail-winged creatures plastered
the lighted windows of stores so thickly it was impossible to see through the glass. The emerging insects
could be seen at dusk arising from the surface of the
water even on the brink of the great falls.

Chapter XVII

INSECT AQUARIUMS

IF YOU want to watch the habits of water insects and observe at close range such interesting things as how a diving beetle pursues its prey, how a dragonfly nymph shoots like a tiny rocket along the bottom of a pond, how a miraculous change turns this hideous creature into the winged and glittering adult, all you have to do is stock an insect aquarium.

You can keep your collection in fish bowls, Mason jars, tin pans, buckets, halves of kegs or old-fashioned wooden washtubs. But, best of all, for watching what is going on, are rectangular glass aquariums. Common round goldfish bowls distort the image and make observation difficult. For insect work, several smaller rectangular cages are better than one large one. You can obtain the right kind of aquariums at any pet store or you can make them yourself.

A convenient size for such an aquarium is fourteen inches long, nine inches wide and eight inches high. To construct such a glass house, you will need the following materials:

One oak board, 16" x 11" x 1½"
Two sheets of glass, double-thick, 14" x 8"
Two sheets of glass, double-thick, 9" x 8"
Four strips of thin glass, 7½" long and 1" wide
Adhesive tape

One inch from the edge of the board, all the way around, cut a groove slightly wider than the thickness of the sheets of glass and one-half inch deep. (See Fig. 18.) This board forms the base of the aquarium

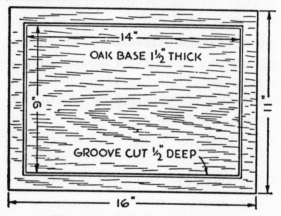

Fig. 18.—Base of Aquarium.

and can be painted any desired color. While the paint is drying, mix up cement, using the following ingredients: One part white sand, one part plaster of Paris, one part litharge, one-third part powdered resin. Adding just enough boiled linseed oil to make a thick paste, stir the mixture until it is smooth and without lumps.

Now you are ready to put together your aquarium. Fill the grooves in the baseboard with the cement and

press the edges of the glass sheets down in place. By
running adhesive tape vertically up each corner on the
outside, to form an additional support, you can hold

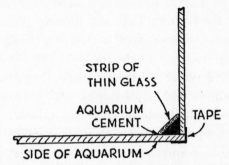

STRIP OF
THIN GLASS

AQUARIUM
CEMENT

TAPE

SIDE OF AQUARIUM

Fig. 19.—Detail of Corner Construction of Aquarium.

the glass box together while you place the narrow glass
strips in each corner and fill the triangular space with
the cement as shown in Fig. 19. When this hardens,
the corners will be watertight and the aquarium will
be ready for use. (See Fig. 20.)

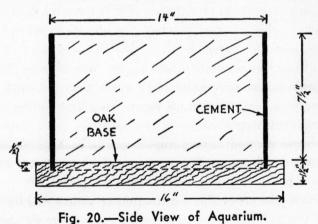

14"

7½"

OAK
BASE

CEMENT

16"

Fig. 20.—Side View of Aquarium.

After you have let the aquarium stand for several days to be sure the cement is hard, fill the glass box with water and then pour it off. Do this several times. Then place a layer of sand, about an inch and a half thick, on the bottom. This will provide anchorage for the growing water plants that will be put in place later on. Be sure to boil or bake the sand before using it to kill bacteria which otherwise might contaminate the water. Pebbles and small stones, which are placed on top of the sand, should be treated similarly.

Fill the aquarium with about five inches of water and place in it sufficient green plants to provide food and to keep the water supplied with oxygen. For this purpose, water cress, eel grass, chara, water crowfoot or similar plants will prove satisfactory. From a pet store, you can obtain some "parrot's feather" to increase the attractiveness of your aquarium. It pays, I have found, to have a few plants with broad leaves on which insects, such as the Hydrophilus beetle, can come to sun themselves. Also, if you have nymphs in the aquarium, be sure you have upright sticks protruding above the water on which the creatures can climb for their transformation into adults. Mosquito-netting or wire-screen covers should be placed over the aquarium to prevent the winged forms from flying away as soon as they appear.

Some of your insect captives will be vegetarian, others carnivorous. The former will be nourished by the plants growing in the aquarium, especially by the roots of the cress. The carnivorous creatures will have

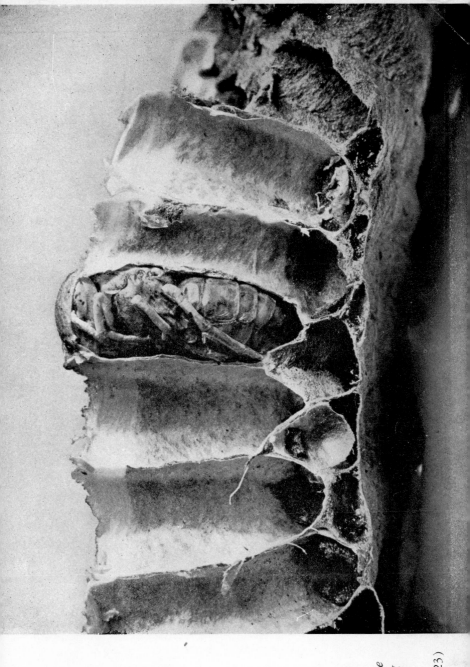

*A young
Hornet
just before
emerging
from its
cell.
(See page 123)*

Dragonflies sleep clinging to the underside of leaves and flowers.
(*See page* 147)

Two Water-Striders darting past a Frog.
(*See page* 150)

Insect hunting in a swamp.
(*See page* 163)

Bees at work filling a comb with honey.
(See page 171)

Hot Weather Bees clinging to the front of a hive.
(See page 173)

The strange Ambush Bug, only a quarter of an inch long, can capture Bumblebees and Butterflies.

(*See page* 189)

Balanced by a clay tail, this injured Dragonfly circled several times around a room.

(*See page 195*)

A Daddy Longlegs of the air—a Crane Fly clinging to grass.
(*See page* 154)

Crickets are often seen in the beam of your flashlight.
(*See page* 208)

An angular-winged Katydid above its eggs attached to a maple twig.

(*See page 210*)

The face of a Locust, or short-horned grasshopper.
(*See page* 210)

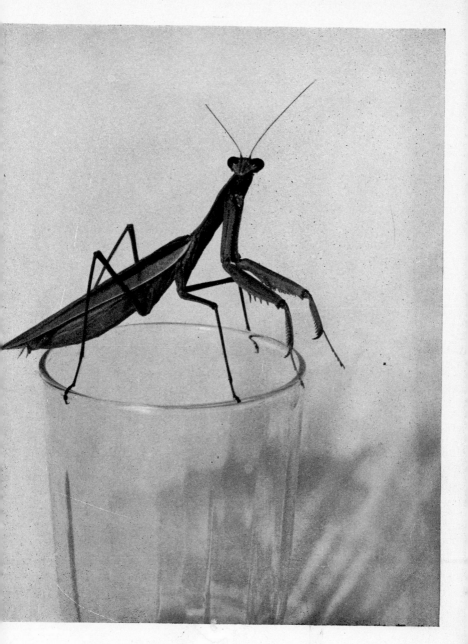

A pet Praying Mantis using five feet to balance itself on the top of a glass.
(*See page 215*)

Butterfly
pets can be
fed on
sugar and
water or
the nectar
of fresh
flowers.
(See page 218)

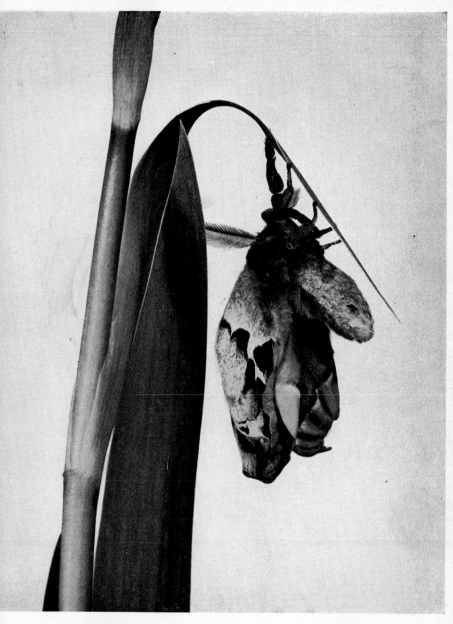

*A Polyphemus Moth unfolding its wings a few minutes after emerging
from the cocoon.*
(*See page* 227)

to be fed smaller insects. They thrive on mosquito larvae and tiny water creatures which you can obtain from any pail of pond water. By sweeping an insect net through long grass and weeds, you can obtain a variety of small insects to drop into the water as food for your aquarium inmates. In winter, feed the carnivorous creatures tiny pieces of meat.

Be careful not to mix carnivorous and plant-eating specimens together—if you want any of the plant-eaters to survive. Also don't put dragonfly nymphs of different sizes together. You will find the smaller ones disappearing, devoured by their cannibal brothers!

The care of the aquarium, once it is established, is relatively simple. Add a snail or two to keep the sides of the glass house free from scum or green algae. If you find the glass becoming green, add more snails and keep the aquarium out of the direct sunlight. The best place for your observation house is in a light corner where it will not be struck by too brilliant sunshine. Keep your aquarium clean. You may need a lifter to remove trash or dead specimens. One can be made easily from a wire and a piece of screen soldered together as shown in Fig. 21. To clean the glass sides occasionally, wrap a piece of flannel around a stick. A trick that helps in removing particles of leaves and bits of waste matter from the sand at the bottom of the aquarium is to employ a one-quarter-inch glass tube. Push the tube down directly over the object while your finger covers the upper end. Then remove your finger. The rush of water up the tube will carry the particle with it. Place your finger over the upper end again and lift tube and particle out. If a film of dust or bacteria forms on the surface of the water, it should be removed as it prevents absorption of air at the surface. This can be done by the use of blotting paper or a newspaper. To prevent such dust scum, place coarse cheesecloth over the aquarium in place of the wire or mosquito netting.

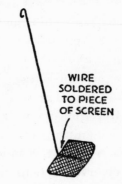

WIRE
SOLDERED
TO PIECE
OF SCREEN

Fig. 21.—Wire Lifter for Removing Trash.

So much for the work of keeping the insect aquarium shipshape. Now for the fun of stocking it. Spring is the best time to collect most of your specimens although in some cases you can find water creatures active in midwinter when almost all other insects are dead or lost to the world in hibernation. Smaller ponds are best for collecting.

When you set out on a trip, take a number of jars and bottles as well as your water net and a small bucket. The net for underwater work should be smaller and stronger than for aerial work. Extra heavy wire should form the ring, about eight inches in diameter, while the net itself should be of strong bobbinet and have the general shape of half a grapefruit rather than the cone-shaped form of the butterfly net. The details of construction are shown in Fig. 22. If you make the net with a demountable handle, have a metal ferrule at the end. If you slip the wood into the joint without such a covering, it will swell in the water and you will have difficulty getting it out until the fibers dry.

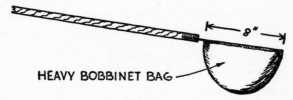

HEAVY BOBBINET BAG

Fig. 22.—Net for Catching Underwater Insects.

In sweeping a pond below the surface, be careful not to scoop up mud. If you move your net along just above the bottom, swirls will pick up any underwater creatures which are resting on the bottom and lift them several inches above the mud. The best place to search for dragonfly nymphs and similar creatures is at the reedy borders of ponds and at points where trash has collected in the eddies of creeks.

Oftentimes, a common garden rake can be used for dragging masses of underwater trash to the shore. An even simpler aid is a ring of barbed wire. This is thrown into weed beds from the shore and pulled in by an attached rope or wire. It often brings clumps of the weeds with it. The ring should be about two or three feet in diameter and it is best to use several loops of the barbed wire.

When you have weeds and trash ashore, place the material on a flat, open space, or better still on a board or white piece of oilcloth. As you sort it over, you will see various creatures wiggling or seeking to work their way back into the water. Place them in the water in your jars or bottles and identify them when you get home. For smaller insects, you can sort over the material you bring up in your net in a light pie tin. The sides prevent the escape of the insects until you can capture them. You will be surprised at the activity shown by some of these underwater dwellers when they are brought ashore.

For capturing specimens in a stream or in a pond where there is no great amount of vegetation, you can use a strip of common screen wire attached to two handles in the manner shown in Fig. 23. Move this along as you would a small seine, lifting it frequently to examine the contents.

In carrying your insects home, it is well to separate them as much as possible. Don't dump them all together in a single pail if you can help it. If you do, you are likely to find that when you get home there will be fewer specimens than when you started. For many of the creatures you will capture are not only carnivorous, they are cannibalistic as well.

An entirely different method of obtaining dragon-

flies is to watch on hot summer days for females laying their eggs. Note where they deposit them, particularly in the stalks of reeds. Break off the stems and
take them home. Or, if you see the female in the act
of ovipositing, you can sometimes capture her and
hold her with the tip of her abdomen in a small bottle

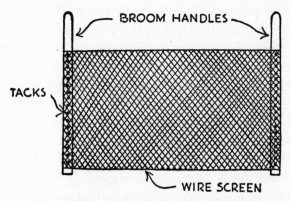

**Fig. 23.—Seine Made from Broomhandles and
Strip of Wire Screen.**

of water. Here she will continue laying the egg masses
and you will have them where they will hatch. However, remember that the water in the bottle must be
dirty! Unless there are bits of decaying vegetable matter, mud or sand in the water the eggs will stick together and get moldy. In from five days to three weeks,
under favorable conditions, however, they break open
and produce midget nymphs. From then on, you can
see the small immature creatures foraging for food
and, if kept together, stalking and devouring each
other.

If you collect partially grown nymphs from ponds or streams, try to get them as nearly full grown as possible. You can tell how far they have developed by the length of the wing cases. As they near maturity they are easier to capture. This is not only because they are larger but because they spend more of their time near the margins of ponds and streams. Most dragon-flies become adults early in the morning, between the beginning of dawn and sunrise. As soon as you get up each morning, look at your aquariums which contain nearly grown nymphs to see if you can find one in the midst of its transformation.

This unforgettable sight—the muddy-colored skin of the nymph splitting down the back and the brilliant rumpled adult working itself slowly free and unfold-ing—well repays the time of watching. While this is probably the most spectacular show that your aquarium will furnish, there are a host of other interesting acts. You will see the curious caddis worms building their tube houses and moving about like animated bits of weed. You will see the whirligig beetles spinning on the surface and the Dytiscus and Hydrophilus diving like insect submarines. The whole strangeness of the underwater life of these small creatures will be ex-posed to your gaze.

Besides indoor aquariums, you can, if you live close to a pond or creek, have fun with outdoor cages in which the nymphs and other underwater creatures live under natural conditions. Roll a strip of galvanized screen in the form of a cylinder, sewing up the side with fine wire, and then push one end down two or three inches into the mud and place a bit of mosquito netting over the top. When you have placed your nymphs in such an outdoor container, visit it every morning. The emerging dragonflies will crawl up the side of the screen out of the water. These cylinders of wire should be about fifteen inches high and six or eight inches in diameter and should protrude five or six inches above the water. The natural vegetation and conditions of the pond bottom will provide food for the nymphs without extra care.

Whether you try outdoor cages or not, stocking a home aquarium will provide plenty of opportunities to watch insect life—in winter as well as in summer. When your other friends of the insect world are gone, many of the strange creatures that spend their days beneath the water will look out at you through glass walls and will carry on their interesting activity a few inches in front of your eyes.

Chapter XVIII

BEES

EVERY boy with a sweet tooth likes honey. It was the world's first candy and the insects that produce it have been prized since long before written history began. In the Seventeenth Century, when colonists came to America, they brought honeybees with them. The Indians had never seen them before and called them "the white man's flies."

Today, the white man's "flies" are familiar in every part of the country. They produce something like 500,000,000 pounds of honey every year in the United States alone. It has been calculated that bees must bring in 37,000 loads of nectar to produce one pound of honey. A colony of bees, each worker making ten trips afield, will visit as many as 300,000 flowers in a day. No wonder the busy bee is celebrated for its industry!

Yet, out of the thousands of kinds of bees known to science, only a few store up honey. The rest live a hand-to-mouth existence, eating nectar where they find it. The hive bees, when storing the nectar in cells, often keep fanning it all night long so a current of air passes over it. By morning a full fourth of the nectar gathered the previous day may have evaporated. But the remaining three-fourths is concentrated sweetness.

In the desert regions of Colorado, honeybees have been seen collecting nectar from flowers so tiny they had to be viewed through a magnifying glass! Most of the marketable honey in the United States comes from about twenty-four kinds of blossoms. White clover leads all the rest, with alfalfa, sweet clover and buckwheat all noted as sources of nectar.

Most honeybees go from one flower to another of the same kind, passing over a host of dissimilar blossoms. Thus, they carry pollen to fertilize plants. Without this aid from bees, most plants would disappear from the earth. The bee pays as it goes, taking nectar and distributing pollen. This work is of more dollar-and-cents value to agriculturists than the honey the bees produce. In the great orchards of the West, colonies of bees are kept, especially to fertilize the fruit-tree blooms. In one of the biggest greenhouses in the country, hives of bees are placed within the glass buildings to carry pollen from plant to plant.

But the bees retain for themselves part of the golden dust which makes plants fertile. To see how they use this pollen let us turn to the remarkable life of the hive, the bee city with its different castes and its amazingly efficient organization.

All the life of the hive centers around the queen and each colony has only one queen. She lays the eggs in the cells produced by the workers, depositing as many as 1,500 in a single day. Out of the eggs hatch the three kinds of bees found in every hive: the workers, the drones, the queens. The workers are normally sterile females that do not mate; the drones are males. As she lays each egg, the queen determines whether it will hatch into a drone or a worker. If it is to become a worker, she fertilizes the egg with sperm-cells from a pocket which was filled by the male during the mating flight. Drones hatch from unfertilized eggs. Queens are produced by the workers when they feed "royal jelly," a milky-white secretion from their head glands, to a certain number of immature workers. This "royal jelly" is also fed to the queen mother of the colony by the "ladies-in-waiting," the attendants that surround and guard her in the hive.

Before the queen lays each egg, the cell is cleaned until it almost shines. Day and night, a number of workers, vibrating their wings to produce a draft, keep the hive ventilated and the brood chamber at a constant temperature of about ninety-three degrees F. Long before man appeared on earth, bees had thus mastered the fundamentals of air conditioning.

Three days after the egg is laid, it hatches into the baby bee. This is a blind, footless grub that eats all day long and increases its weight as much as 1,500 times in six days. At the end of that time, it spins a cocoon and the workers outside, which have been feeding it a mixture of pollen and honey, place a porous cap over the cell. From 16 to 24 days after the egg is laid, the fully developed bee bites its way out of the cell and joins in the work of the hive. Drones require 24 days to reach maturity, workers 21 days and queens only 16.

For the first week or so, the young bee labors in the hive, then it makes its initial flights afield. On these first trips it gathers either water or propolis, the resinous "bee glue" obtained from trees and used for smoothing over rough places in the hive. The next duty is collecting pollen and the final work is gathering nectar. The pollen is kneaded into a ball and carried home in the insect's "pollen basket," a little cavity on the bee's hind leg. Nectar is obtained by protruding the tongue into the flower and sucking the sweet fluid into the mouth and on into the "honey bag" in which it is carried back to the wax cells of the comb.

These wax cells have been called one of the wonders of the world. They are produced from whitish material coming from tiny pockets on the bee's abdomen. The workers chew this waxy secretion into a soft paste which is molded with their jaws into the tissue-paper-thin walls—often only 1-180th of an inch thick —which form the sides of the cells. In spite of the frail appearance of the combs, they can support surprising weights. Tests have shown that a honeycomb is capable of supporting a weight thirty times its own.

In summer, a danger faced by the bees is the melting of the wax. This would permit the honey to run out of its sealed containers. Corps of fanning insects, gripping with their feet and moving their wings so fast they are visible only as a blur, send a steady stream of cooling air through the hive.

Only the queen and those workers born late in the summer live over the winter. The average life of a worker during the hardest labor of summer is about six weeks. By the end of that time, they have literally worked themselves to death. Queens, unless they are accidentally killed, may live for four or five years or even longer. The drones all die in that strange massacre in which the workers turn on these lazy males after they have served their purpose by fertilizing the young queens.

These queens come from the largest cells constructed in the hive. Often such birth chambers look like small peanuts. The first queen to hatch immediately tears open the other queen cells and stings to death the inmates, thus getting rid of all her rivals for leadership. Unlike worker bees, queens can sting again and again. When a worker bee stings you, to adapt the old phrase of fathers in the woodshed, "it hurts them more than it does you." For they commit suicide when they sting. The barbed sting is torn out, causing death afterwards. To use this sting, a bee has to employ twenty-two different muscles. Queens, which can sting again and again, never attack man. And the drones possess no stings to use.

A curious thing in connection with bee stings is the fact that many medical men believe the venom which is injected is valuable in curing rheumatism. A man who says he has been cured in this way maintains a special apiary in Minnesota where he offers free stings to sufferers from rheumatism!

One of the strangest events in the life of the hive is

the swarming, which takes place early in summer. It is a sort of Fourth of July for the bees. It is their one vacation from toil; a curious mass picnic. All the bees seem happy. They almost never sting when swarming. They gorge themselves with honey before the start and have no desire for food. Following the queen, they leave the old hive—on the great adventure of their lives.

The swarm always takes place when there are several large queen cells present in the hive. Whether the old queen leaves to get away from these coming rivals or whether the swarm is driven on by a desire to found a new home, no one knows. But always, thousands of bees appear outside the hive, usually between ten and twelve o'clock on a bright morning, flying around and around and finally alighting on some limb or post, forming a ball of living insects. After the swarm settles, scout bees fly away in all directions looking for a new home. If the beekeeper can shake the mass into a basket and transport it to an empty hive, the insects will welcome the offered home. If this is not done, the bees, instructed in some mysterious manner by the scouts, rise in a great whirling ball, ten or twenty feet in diameter, and sail away over trees and houses to a home which the pioneer bees have located. It is sometimes an attic, or inside a loose wall or in a hollow tree. All wild bees, found in hollow trees in woods, were originally swarms that escaped from hives and "went native." The bumblebees, but not the honeybees, are native to America. All American honeybees are descendants of insects originally imported from abroad.

Back at the old hive, left by the swarm, the first queen to hatch kills her rivals and becomes leader of the colony growing up in the deserted home. Before settling down to egg laying, she makes a spectacular mating flight. Soaring up and up, followed by a trail of drones, she mates with the strongest, high in the heavens. The drone dies almost instantly and his dead body falls to earth, turning over and over. The queen, however, returns to the hive where everything centers around her. If anything happens to the queen, the colony becomes disorganized. It has been suggested that the odor she gives off has a calming and reassuring effect on the workers.

Like the ants, bees appear to recognize other members of their colony by smell. When bee-keepers wish to introduce a new queen in a hive, they often follow a peculiar procedure. If they placed her among the workers before she gained the odor of the hive, these insects would attack and kill her. So she is inserted in a small protecting wire cage, the doorway of which is stopped up by a plug of candy. By the time the bees have gnawed their way through this sweet material, the queen inside has taken on the hive odor and she is accepted without question by the members of the colony.

A somewhat similar method is employed for joining two colonies that are too weak to survive a winter or produce a good crop of honey. If bees of a different odor were placed together, they would fall on each other in a desperate life-or-death battle. But, by placing one hive on top of the other, with a sheet of newspaper between, the apiary owner accomplishes the desired result. Gradually the bees gnaw little holes in the paper. Through these openings the two hive odors intermingle. By the time the holes are big enough to permit the insects to pass through, the latter have a common odor and accept each other without hostility.

Sometimes, a queen on returning from a mating flight gets into the wrong hive. The result is a death battle for supremacy between the two queens. Observers have reported that the workers do not interfere unless the combatants get into a position where both are apt to be killed. Then, the workers separate the queens, letting them come to grips again till one is victor. Whichever it is, the conquering queen is accepted as leader of the hive.

It is a curious thing that while man has domesticated dogs and cats, sheep and cattle, horses and chickens, rabbits and pigs, to mention but a few animals, hardly any of all the hundreds of thousands of insects have been domesticated. The silkworm—larva of a moth— and the honeybee are the outstanding examples. Of the two, the life of the bee, with its complex cities of wax, its castes and division of duties, is the more interesting. The next chapter will tell you how you can keep and observe these insects, watching through glass windows the fascinating life of the hive.

Chapter XIX

KEEPING BEES

SOME years ago, a boy in Ohio put himself through college by keeping bees. He didn't take his insects to school with him like Mary's little lamb. But he did take the honey they produced and he sold it at a good profit.

Bees require comparatively little care. You don't have to feed and water them. You don't have to bed them down for the night. You don't have to exercise them. If you provide the correct kind of hive and observe a few simple rules, the insects will do the rest. The old saying is: "They work for nothing and board themselves." Even in town, you can keep a hive of honeybees in the backyard. The insects will fly afield, finding their own pastures.

The best bees to begin with are the Italian strains. They are milder in temper and can be handled more easily by an amateur. You can purchase a swarm of these bees for approximately five dollars from a local bee-keeper or an apiary supply house. It is best to purchase the hive and other necessary equipment ready-made. Later on, if you desire, you can construct other hives of the same pattern. Complete with movable frames, such a hive will cost approximately as much as the bees to stock it. In good years, the honey from a single hive will bring in a return of from three to five dollars.

The best plan is to disturb your bees as little as possible. Midday, when the sun is hottest, is the best time for handling the insects. Never, unless it is absolutely necessary, disturb them at night or in wet weather. Wear a bee veil, to protect your face, and force smoke into the hive with a smoker before you begin work. Make your motions deliberate and try to avoid jarring the hive. While most bee-keepers become immune to the poison of the stings, the odor of the formic acid which the stinging insects inject excites the swarm and makes it difficult to manage. The best way to remove a sting is by scraping it out with a knife or your fingernail. In this way, you do not squeeze the poison sac which is usually attached to the sting when it pulls away from the body of the bee.

When bees swarm, you often can walk right into the swirling cloud of insects. When they alight on some branch, shake the whole cluster down into a box or basket and carry it quickly to a vacant hive. Once placed in front of the door, the insects almost invariably march inside and set up housekeeping in their new home. Thereafter, only a few simple rules must be observed.

For example, keep the grass cut around the hive. This will prevent the bees from becoming entangled when they return from the fields with their loads of honey. The hives should be placed so they are in shade part of the day during the heat of summer. In fall, when the combs of honey are removed, from twenty-five to thirty pounds should be left in the brood chamber to feed the bees and keep them alive during the winter. To protect the inmates from the cold, larger boxes should be placed around the hives, leaving a small opening so the bees can get out in fine weather. Sometimes, the space between box and hive is filled with chaff to help insulate the swarm against the cold. This method of protecting the bees is usually far better than bringing the hives into the cellar during the months of cold.

These are some of the fundamental rules for the bee-keeper. Special problems in connection with the work are beyond the scope of this book. At the start, it will pay you to make the acquaintance of a local bee-keeper. He will be glad to explain how he carries on his work and he will aid you when you meet special problems in connection with caring for the hives. Also, several texts on "bee farming" given at the end of this book should prove valuable.

While most of us will never turn to bee-keeping as a livelihood, we can have great sport and see a good many interesting things by stocking an observation hive. A beehive with a transparent wall permits you to see all the fascinating activity within just as we saw the home life of the ants by making a glass-walled ant house. At leading apiary supply houses, such as the A. I. Root Company, at Medina, O., you can purchase a small observation hive, already stocked with bees, for five dollars or less. Or, if you can obtain a conventional hive, you can turn it into a "house with a glass wall" without great difficulty.

Simply cut a rectangular section out of one side and use this piece of wood for a door, hinged at the bottom and held closed at the top. Across this opening, on the inside, place a pane of clear glass. As in all observation houses, be sure the glass is free from "knots" and other imperfections which will distort the image.

Such a hive can be kept indoors with a runway leading out through a crack in a window. The rest of the crack should be closed with a screen or a piece of wood to prevent the insects from entering the room itself. For summer months, a window facing the east is usually best. However, the exit-window should never face directly into the prevailing wind as bees in a drafty observation-hive never do well.

When you have finished watching the events within the hive, always close the door. Bees dislike much light inside the hive and if you leave the door open too long they will "pull down the shade," that is, coat over the pane with dark propolis or bee glue. They obtain this material from trees, especially from leaf buds. It is used both to stop up cracks and to smooth over rough places within the hive.

With your observation-hive ready, you can follow through the year's activity of the insect swarm. You may see the queen laying her eggs; the workers coming and going, bringing in their loads of nectar, pollen and bee glue; the drones—burly fellows with enormous eyes and long wings—crawling about within the hive.

You may be able to follow through the whole lifecycle of the workers. You will see the older bees molding the wax by means of their jaws, into the cells which form the cradles. Then comes the pollen, carried by workers in tiny "baskets" on the outer sides of their rear legs. Sometimes these baskets will be packed so full, they look like small boxing gloves going around and around, as though in a sparring match, as the insect rapidly moves its legs. The pollen is packed into the cells by workers which use their heads as ramrods to force the fluffy golden material into place. Mixed with honey, it is called bee bread. On an edible mattress of this kind, the queen lays her eggs. Then the cells are capped over with wax. From 16 to 24 days after the egg is laid, the hatching insects bite their way through the cell caps and enter the world of the hive.

If any of the bees die, you will see their bodies carefully removed. All waste matter is carried out of the hive, for bees are scrupulously clean housekeepers. If you place a bit of meat in the hive, too large to remove, the insects will cover it over carefully with bee glue. The individual insects spend much of their time cleaning themselves with tongue and legs. On the front legs of the workers, you will notice little antennae cleaners, through which they run their feelers to remove dust and dirt.

In midsummer, when the workers are streaming in and out, you will see a few insects standing still, beating their wings until they are merely a blur. They are the "electric fans" that keep the interior of the hive from becoming overheated. Sometimes, you will see two of the insects locked in a desperate battle inside the hive. This means that a robber bee has entered to steal honey. You can help the insects of your hive to protect their stores under such conditions by stopping up the doorway so no more than one bee at a time can gain entrance. This will make it more difficult for the robbers to get past the guardian bees and into the hive.

During September, you may witness that strange occurrence, the murder of the males. After the young queens and drones have made their mating flight, the workers of the hive, which have tenderly fed and cared for the males all summer, turn on them, drive them out, and slay them. The mating season being over, the drones are no longer of use in Nature's plan.

Occasionally, while winter winds blow, you can peep into your hive. You will find the bees clustered together, inactive for the most part, apparently taking a needed rest after the bustle of summer months.

While you are watching the activity of the year inside your observation-hive, you can add to the fun by making experiments that show the amazing way in which the insect community is organized. Blow a little dust or flour into the hive and you will see workers busy cleaning up and removing all the particles. Put saucers about the yard holding a little honey or syrup stained with candy coloring fluids. Note which color has the most bees around it and see if the bees mix the colors or keep them separate in placing the fluid in the cells. By daubing spots of colored lacquer on the backs of several of the bees, you can often recognize them again.

It was by marking honeybees in this manner that the famous European scientist, Dr. Karl von Frisch, carried on the researches that led to his dramatic discovery of the "language of the bees." In 1949, when von Frisch visited America, I saw his moving pictures of marked bees on the comb of an observation hive. They revealed how workers that have found a rich source of nectar in the field return home and perform a peculiar tail-wagging dance on the honeycomb. Other workers crowd around these scout bees. By variations in the form and character of the dance, the scouts appear able to indicate the direction, the bearing in relation to the sun and even the distance of the nectar-filled flowers. The record of von Frisch's experiments is given in detail in his book, *Bees, Their Vision, Chemical Senses, and Language*, published by Cornell University in 1951. It is one of the great adventure stories of insect research.

Chapter XX

THE REAL BUGS

THERE is an old story about two boys who tried to fool their teacher. They glued the head of a cicada on the body of a grasshopper and added the wings of a butterfly. When they brought the result to class for identification, the teacher said:

"This is the queerest bug I ever saw. I will examine it closely tonight and in the morning I will let you know what it is."

The next day, the whole class arrived early.

"I have identified your bug," the teacher announced. "It is a *humbug!*"

Many of the real bugs you will meet in your insect-hunting live such strange lives that they, also, may seem like humbugs. But, they will be living creatures, honest-to-goodness insects that it will pay you to study.

In the first place, a good many "bugs" are not bugs at all. "Lightning bugs" aren't bugs; "Potato bugs" aren't bugs; "Ladybugs" aren't bugs; "June bugs" aren't bugs. They are all beetles and beetles have biting mouth-parts while the distinguishing characteristic of a bug is a sucking beak.

The biggest of the bugs is the noisy cicada. Since the

days of the Pilgrim fathers, who mistook the emergence of the periodical insects for a plague of Biblical locusts, the cicadas have been called "locusts."

Under the bases of the wings of the cicada males are the round drums with which they make their shrill, resounding call. The drum consists of a corrugated membrane suggesting a washing board. This membrane is set in rapid motion by special muscles. The effect is something like bending the bottom of a tin pan in and out rapidly. The females have no drums. But they do have a curious implement beneath their abdomens. It is a chisel-like ovipositor looking something like the tailskid on an airplane. With it, they slice openings in the twigs of various trees and in these slits insert their eggs.

Out of the eggs hatch pale, antlike creatures which drop to the ground and burrow below the surface. Here they remain for from one to seventeen years, according to the species. They feed on the sap of rootlets and as they grow, shed their skins. The last molt occurs above ground, when the cicadas become shining, winged creatures of the air and sunshine after their long imprisonment in an insect underworld.

More common are the cicadas which appear each summer. You can tell when you have a periodical cicada by its red eyes and the red-yellow veins on its wings. The most common yearly species is greenish and lacks the more brilliant coloration of its relative— the Rip Van Winkle of the insect world.

From the biggest bug, let us jump to one of the

smallest. Out in the fields, you have often seen in early summer masses of white froth clinging to the stems of weeds and grasses. Each mass is the foam-castle of the curious frog hopper, or spittle insect. Using a piece of grass-stem, poke the froth and you soon will uncover a chubby little greenish-yellow creature, a quarter of an inch or so in length. It will run down the stem of the plant on frail, hairlike legs. It soon stops, however, thrusts its sharp little beak into the tissues of the plant and begins pumping out the juices. At the same time, its pointed tail begins waving from side to side, beating fluid which it gives off into a froth suggestive of the whipped white of an egg. Always, these clever little fellows hang head downward so gravity pulls the accumulating mass of froth down over their bodies. Within such a mass, the immature insect lives, protected from the heat of the sun and the jaws and stings of its enemies. On reaching maturity, it develops wings and flies away.

Among the other minute members of the bug family which employ their needle-sharp beaks to drain away plant juices are the tree hoppers. Oftentimes these midgets have grotesque little bodies which have given them the name of "the insect brownies." Some appear to be wearing queer hats, others resemble seeds and thorns and miniature bisons. When you approach or touch one of these hoppers, it springs into the air as though shot aloft by a soundless explosion.

In spite of their small size, still another kind of tiny bug, the leaf hoppers, causes considerable loss. A million leaf hoppers may live on a single acre of pasture grass. And, their combined appetites, by draining away vital plant juices, will destroy as much grass as a cow will eat.

Other drinkers of plant sap do even more damage. They are the aphides or plant lice which, as we have seen, are the milk-cows of the ants. Oftenest, the aphides are green. But I have found close-packed masses of yellow, red, black and patterned members of this branch of the bug clan. The life of these creatures is as fantastic as a story from the *Arabian Nights*.

For instance, they multiply so fast that one scientist has calculated that if all natural checks were removed and all the descendants of a single female aphis lived, at the end of one summer season the progeny of this original female would weigh more than all the people on earth! And these individual aphides are so small that it takes sixty to weigh as much as a kernel of wheat!

Generation after generation, during the summer, the females give birth to living young, all females. They in turn, in a few days, begin adding to the aphis population of the plant on which they find themselves. Thus a rose shoot will be covered with a solid mass of the insects, all pumping out sap through their little beaks. Every so often, before the flowing rivers of plant juice can give out, a generation with wings appears. These winged insects sail away to found new colonies on other plants. Sometimes, carried by the wind, they sail for many miles. When autumn comes, males are born. These mate with females and the latter lay eggs which hatch out the following spring.

The thick masses of the aphides form a sort of pasture on which many carnivorous insects feed. One of the most ravenous is the tiny, lizard-shaped aphis lion. It is the larva of the lacewing fly. The mother fly has to place her eggs high on slender stalks so the first aphis lion to hatch will not devour its brothers and sisters before they can get free from their restraining shells. This bloodthirsty little creature runs from one aphis to another, piercing their sides with its sharp jaws and letting the life-juices trickle down its throat until only the empty, puckered-up bag of the plant louse's body remains. It has been seen killing an aphis a minute in this way.

As strange as anything in the life of the aphis is the method it sometimes uses for warding off attacks. It "gums up" the enemy by pushing glue into its face!

If you examine one of these creatures closely, you will see two short tubes slanting upward from the back of its rotund body. Out of them, the insects can exude a mass of waxy glue which it thrusts into the face of an approaching foe. The glue dries almost instantly and the attacking insect has to stop and clean the wax away. While it is doing this, the aphis can move out of danger. This strange maneuver is the plant louse's only means of defense.

A paradoxical thing about one branch of the bug clan is the fact that its members combine beautiful colors and vile smells. Before you go far in insect exploring, you will meet flat, shield-shaped insects—the stink bugs. One common insect of this kind is found in cabbage fields. Its body is shiny black or deep blue with striking red markings. It has various names such as calico bug, terrapin bug and fire bug. But it is most widely known as the Harlequin cabbage bug. The females lay their eggs usually six in a row and twelve eggs in a place. Each egg resembles a tiny beer keg, complete even to the hoops and bung!

Squash bugs also have an unpleasant odor and a few have curious habits that make them especially interesting. One kind, for example, has a depression surrounded by spines on its back. In this fenced-in area, the male carries the eggs deposited by the female.

Neither the cabbage bug nor the squash bug approaches the chinch bug as an agricultural pest. This midget, between one-sixteenth and one-half inch long when full-grown, has caused more than $500,000,000 worth of damage on American farms. A blackish insect with white wings and reddish legs, it feeds on the sap of corn, hay and grain. Sometimes, in infested fields, the insects are so numerous that they completely hide whole stalks of growing corn.

Burrowing bugs, with flattened front feet for digging; assassin—or kissing—bugs, which do good by killing potato beetles; thread-legged bugs—delicate creatures suggesting frail walking sticks which live under loose bark and in tufts of grass, are other unusual members of the bug tribe.

Among all the varied members of this clan, however, the one—besides the aphis—which has afforded me the most interesting hours is the strange and fearful little ambush bug. About half an inch long, it has green, brown and black markings and yellowish eyes. Its back seems covered with crinkled and horny armor. Its little feelers end in enlarged knobs that suggest the grips on the handlebars of a velocipede. Its forelegs are equipped with long claws which are carried at rest folded back into streamlined appendages which resemble the "pants" on the wheels of a racing airplane. To complete its bizarre body, there is a tiny poison beak that folds back under its head when not in use.

With its claws and beak, it takes a position on some flower and awaits its prey. I have seen it capture bees, bumblebees, butterflies—the latter many times its size. A few convulsive flaps of the wings and the insect victim hangs motionless while the ambush bug sucks out the body juices. Once, I found a large bee, a white cabbage butterfly and two Red Admiral butterflies all dangling from the blooms of a single buddleia bush, all grasped by these little monsters in miniature. Although they are deadly to insects, the ambush bugs are harmless to man.

When one flower dries up, the ambush bug spreads its little wings and sails away to a new hiding place in some other bloom. You will find them, along with crab spiders, often clinging silently among the petals of some clump of small blossoms. If you have a magnifying glass, watch the movements of this curious bug closely. Its complete life story is unknown. As is the case among so many six-legged creatures, there remains much investigation to be done in connection with this curious midget before we know all the interesting things it has to tell us.

Chapter XXI

INSECT EXPERIMENTS YOU CAN MAKE

The words you read in this chapter are being written before breakfast on the Fourth of July. Already the pop and bang of firecrackers comes through the open windows. The noise will continue far into the night. It means excitement for boys and, queerly enough, for lightning bugs as well!

A few years ago, a scientist at Albany, Dr. Rudolph Rudemann, of the New York State Museum, made a surprising discovery about firecrackers and fireflies. Whenever a cracker exploded in the darkness, Dr. Rudemann noticed, lightning bugs flashed on their lights in response. The bigger the firecracker, the bigger the response. A small explosion made about a dozen insects flash on their lights in an area some twenty feet square. A cannon cracker, however, brought a response from forty or fifty of the insects. Each of the explosions "turned on the lights" of the beetles instantly and their flashing continued longer than under ordinary conditions.

The next time the Fourth of July comes around, save some of your firecrackers until after dark and see if you can make the lightning bugs go into action in a similar way. This is one of many interesting experiments with insects you can perform. As suggestions, I am listing a few in this chapter. You will think of others as you go along. Keep careful record and check your results by additional tests.

Here is a second experiment you can make with lightning bugs. Flash a common hand flashlight upward from the grass. Will the flying insects respond to its beam as it goes on and off?

A few insects are said to be deaf. Fabre even shot off a cannon near some of these six-legged creatures and reported they paid no attention to the roar. Are ants deaf? You can blow a horn or shoot off a firecracker near by and see if they show any signs of hearing. Be careful that no vibrations are produced on the insect's support or what you think is hearing may be the result of feeling the tremors.

At night, moths are attracted to lights. Where there are neon signs of several colors, notice if any one attracts more insects than the others. Some observers have reported that blue neons are the favorite.

Another test you can make in connection with color is this: Place little dabs of honey on pieces of paper which are of different colors. Have one bright red, another bright blue, a third green and a fourth yellow. Bees will find the honey. See if they come to any one color more often than to the other colors.

By putting tiny markings with quick-drying lacquer on the backs of ants and bees and other insects, you can recognize the same individuals time after time. You can tell if they return to the same source of supply on return trips.

Similarly, you can mark an ant which you find out foraging not far from a nest and then place near it a bit of meat or a dead insect. Watch it go for help. Does it lead the other workers back to the find or do they find the meat by following the trail left by the marked ant?

Watch the path a marked ant takes out from the nest in search of food. Place a bit of meat in front of it and then see if it follows exactly the same path back to the nest or if it takes a "beeline" home.

Take marked bees and wasps different distances from home and see if they are able to find their way back. How far can they be taken and still return home?

Time the speed of different insects. How long does it take an ant climbing a tree to cover a measured foot or yard? Can ants make more speed on level ground than in climbing or can they go vertically as fast as horizontally?

Time insects at different temperatures and see how their speed varies with heat and cold.

Break the trail left by an ant with onions, perfume, ammonia and other strong-smelling fluids and see if the ants, following the path, are thrown off the trail at these points.

How far can different insects see? Wave a white butterfly net at varying distances in front of different insects and see how close you must get to frighten

them. Which has the farthest sight? Among the butterflies, for instance, which can see the farthest?

How many times their own length can grasshoppers
and crickets jump? Measure a jump and compute the
answer by dividing the jumping distance by the length
of the insect.

How much can a flying insect lift? You can experiment by sticking tiny balls of gum to the feet of dragonflies and other insects, weighing the heaviest balls that
the winged creatures can carry into the air. Such tests
are best carried on indoors where the air is still and
where you can catch the insects to remove the gum
afterwards.

Feed a captured dragonfly or other carnivorous insect in captivity. How many flies or other small insects
will it consume in an hour?

When cicadas and dragonflies molt and become
adults, the shells from which they emerge are anchored
firmly to some reed or twig. How solidly are the shells
attached? With sensitive scales such as are used to
weigh letters, you can pull until the shells break loose,
or you can attach a little sling to a shell and keep
adding BB shot until the shell pull away. How many
times the weight of the insect which emerged is the
pull needed to dislodge the shell? In other words, what
is the "factor of safety" in the anchorage of the shell?

Sometimes, when you find an injured insect, you
can learn surprising things before you drop it into your
killing jar. Once, just as I made a swoop at a dragonfly,
it darted upward and the rim of the net struck it with

such violence it knocked off the insect's abdomen just behind the wings. The dragonfly was still alive and trying to fly. But it had no tail to balance it in the air. I molded a tiny spindle of clay and stuck it on the dragonfly to replace the lost abdomen. Balanced in this way, it sailed for several minutes about a room as though nothing had happened. Another time, I found a dragonfly with one wingtip injured so that it was unable to fly. Before I killed it, I clipped, little by little, the wingtips on both sides until I found that the insect could support itself in the air with wings hardly more than half as long as they normally are.

Near a busy ants' nest, you can make a simple experiment that is interesting to watch. Cut up a dead caterpillar or insect into three pieces, of different sizes. Drop them where lone workers will discover them and then return to the nest for help. Note the number of ants that come to each piece of meat. Do more come to the big pieces than to the little ones?

A record of the results of these and other experiments, if carefully made, will be of real value. As Fabre says, we talk to the insects and interview them through the language of experiment. Learning to talk this language will increase immensely the fun of insect watching.

Chapter XXII

FLIES

IN OTHER chapters of this book, you have made the acquaintance of several members of the Fly tribe. Our commonest pests, the houseflies, gnats and mosquitoes, are found in this group. All are members of the *Diptera* order. The name means "two-winged." All true flies have only one pair of wings with small, knobbed "balancers" behind them in place of a second pair.

The midgets and the giants among these insects are the minute gnats and "no-see-ums" representing the former and the big black or reddish brown horseflies, fully an inch in length, representing the latter. The great compound eyes of the horseflies cover their heads almost like a football helmet. A curious thing about the gnats is the way the males find the females. Tense membranes at the ends of some of the female breathing tubes produce a shrill note when the insect flies. This note sets the hairs on the male's bushy antennae vibrating. Tests have shown that it turns its head in the direction of the sound and thus finds its mate in the dark. Mosquitoes seem to have a similar system of signaling. It is said, if you produce the female's note by means of a tuning fork while watching the antennae of a male under a microscope, you will see the hairs on the side toward the source of the sound begin to quiver.

Altogether, about 40,000 kinds of flies have been described by scientists. Their life story has four chapters. The eggs, or "nits," are laid by the female. In a few days, they hatch into tiny larvae which are variously called maggots, bots or wigglers. Growing rapidly, these larvae mature in a few days. Then comes the most curious part of their history. Many of them dissolve almost completely within their skins and this fluid alters to a sort of jelly which in turn hardens into the body and organs of the adult fly. All this amazing transformation occupies but a few days.

The most rapid reproduction of all is probably among the tiny fruit flies. Place some decaying apples or overripe bananas in the yard, and they will soon attract a swarm of minute winged and yellow insects with pink eyes and banded abdomens. In the laboratories of scientists these midget fruit flies are raised to study heredity as they produce as many as twenty generations in a single year. Put a few in a bottle with a bit of banana, set the container away and a few weeks later note how the fly population has increased. Another interesting experiment you can make with these creatures is to place the bottle in a room where there is only one window admitting light. Note how all the adult flies flock to the lighted side of their prison. Each time you turn the bottle, you will see them move to the side nearest the light.

At a research laboratory in New York, Dr. Frank E. Lutz once showed that these frail and tiny insects are literally "wonder creatures," able to endure strains that would be fatal to the strongest humans. He placed ten flies in a bell jar and sucked out the air until the pressure within was less than that *seventeen miles* above the earth's surface. This is three times the height of Mount Everest, far higher than any stratosphere balloonist has ever gone sealed in his airtight ball. Yet, these flies, without any protection, endured the near-vacuum within the bell jar and were walking about as though nothing had happened four minutes after their release! Twenty-four times in four hours, the same flies went through the same ordeal. Two of the ten not only survived the strains of the "torture chamber" but produced families afterwards!

Sometime when you have nothing to do, try to wear out a housefly by keeping it on the wing. In a closed room, frighten it whenever it starts to alight so that it has to keep going. You will find that you will wear out before the fly! Nobody knows how far or how long a fly can keep on the wing. But, travelers have seen these small insects flying along beside a ship, many miles out at sea.

The manner in which one fly remains on the wing has given it its name. The hover fly is often seen apparently hanging in the air above the flowers of some sunny corner in a garden. Some of these insects have forms and colorings that mimic honeybees, some that mimic bumblebees and some that mimic small wasps.

It was the honeybee-imitators that gave rise to a story which persisted for centuries. This was the belief that honeybees were formed from the carcass of a dead horse or donkey. The flies lay their eggs in decaying meat. When early people saw the swarms of beelike insects hatching from the body of a dead animal, they took for granted they were witnessing the birth of a honeybee colony.

Once, years ago, as a boy in Illinois, I entered a fly-killing contest, seeking a prize offered by the local health department. I was getting along famously until my mother discovered I was spending most of my time crouching near a dead toad in the alley, awaiting the flies as they alighted on it!

Most of these insects, I now know, were members of that loud-humming, brilliant blue or green tribe, the blowflies. These scavenger flies are among the insects that help remove decaying animals from the earth. With the burying beetles and the carrion beetles, their unappetizing efforts really make this a cleaner world in which to live. In their humble way they are doing good work in the world. Of course, their sole aim is to deposit their eggs where the hatching maggots will have food. As many as 20,000 eggs are said to be deposited by a single female blowfly. In some species, the eggs hatch in the body of the female and she lays living larvae instead of eggs. In recent years, surgeons have been using the larvae of blowflies to clean out festering wounds and help patients recover from bone injuries.

If you have ever been bitten by a green-headed horsefly while in swimming, you will have no difficulty remembering the sensation. Like the mosquitoes, only the female horseflies bite. Male horseflies and gadflies are content to sip nectar from flowers while their bloodthirsty mates are seeking living prey. All spend their early days in the water or in moist ground.

Rotting wood is the early home of the fierce hawk-like robber flies. The larvae crawl about in this material seeking other smaller larvae for their food. The adults are streamlined "insect falcons." I have spent hours watching them hawking about over grass and weeds, swooping down on some flying insect, wrapping their long, hooked legs about its body and carrying it to a twig or weed where they calmly drained away its vital juices. Almost all of these flies have long tapering bodies and great eyes covering most of their heads. They suggest racing airplanes. A few are extremely hairy and one kind is easily mistaken for a bumblebee. The insects have varied colors. A common type is frosty gray and yellowish brown.

Toward evening, when the sunlight is slanting under trees, you will find robber flies perched on weed-tops or twigs watching for victims. A swoop and the hawklike creature returns to its perch to dine on its prey. So intent is the insect on its meal that sometimes I have moved my forefinger slowly up under a dining robber fly until it touched the twig. Once, one stepped off on my fingertip and rode along for a dozen yards, still sucking away on a tiny wasp. I could see the abdomen of the victim flattening out like an empty bag. In the horny beak that projects from the face of the robber fly, like a long and pointed nose, is a sliding lancet which cuts through the shell of the victim's body. As this is being done, the fly injects an anesthetic fluid that halts the struggles of the victim.

I have seen these hunters catching moths, scorpion flies, wasps, mosquitoes and many other of the smaller aerial insects. Sometimes, the robber will swoop several times before it grasps its prey. But, usually one strike is sufficient. Some of the largest of these predatory insects are fully an inch in length. A few haunt apiaries and dine on the blood of honeybees. At times, they become a serious menace to bee-keepers. Small piles of empty insect bodies are frequently found under favorite perches of these robber flies.

I remember one reddish-brown robber, which once entertained me for a quarter of an hour with its acrobatics. I first saw it hanging from an over-arching grass blade. With one leg thrust up above its body, it clung to the grass while its other legs were engaged in grasping a large mosquito. I bent too near and frightened it away to another grass blade. It alighted just as before, hanging by one up-reaching "hand," like a boy on a horizontal bar. Three times I alarmed it and, every time, it swooped to another bending blade of grass and took up exactly the same position.

Few insects have the ravenous appetites of the robber flies. In less than an hour, one fly killed and sucked dry eight moths. Seemingly afraid of nothing, the insects will attack and subdue stinging wasps and bees. Sometimes they even capture small dragonflies.

All in all, the fly tribe costs us millions of dollars. We have to buy screens to keep out mosquitoes, fly-paper to catch or poison houseflies, barrels of oil to cover swamps to kill larvae and make life livable in summer months. The Hessian fly, said to have caused American farmers more damage than any other single insect, is estimated to have run up a total of $100,-000,000 damage by 1900. It attacks wheat, rye and barley, destroying about one-tenth of the entire American crop each year. It was introduced in the bedding of the Hessian soldiers who came to America at the time of the Revolution; hence its name. Other flies, such as a parasite which attacks Japanese beetles, are fighting on man's side. But most insects of the kind must be listed among our six-legged enemies. However, pests or not, they are strange and interesting creatures, always close at hand for us to watch.

Chapter XXIII

HUNTING WITH A FLASHLIGHT

WHEN the sun goes down, most of the familiar insects disappear. But a whole new population of less familiar six-legged creatures takes their place. In the darkness, the crickets, katydids, moths, beetles, fireflies and walking sticks come to life.

Usually, we realize only vaguely that they are there. We hear the night orchestra of the katydids, tree crickets and grasshoppers. We see the fireflies in the darkness and the moths and beetles bumping against the windowpane or wheeling about the street lamps. But, as a whole, the nocturnal insects remain indistinct in our minds.

Exploring at night, hunting with a flashlight, is a fascinating sport that will teach us much about these after-dark neighbors of the insect world. Any weed-patch, any backyard, any corner of a garden will provide a hunting ground. And any sort of an electric torch will provide a spotlight that will illuminate the doings of the shy and furtive insects whose day begins with dusk.

There are two ways to hunt with a flashlight. You can sit still and listen for near-by chirps or movements, flashing your beam on the spots from which they come. Or, you can roam about, shooting your spotlight here and there in search of quarry. I have spent hours on summer nights exploring the darkness in these ways. It is curious how the rest of the world seems blotted out, all except the small circle illuminated by your flash-lamp. And here, like actors on a stage, the various insects play their parts.

Late-summer nights, in August and early September, are best. The insect population is at its height and most of the individuals have reached their maturity. Move slowly and cautiously. Make as little noise as possible. When you are tracking down a night insect which makes an audible sound, move a step or two and then wait a few moments before advancing again. After you have made several of these nocturnal hunting expeditions, you will learn where to look for the different kinds of insects. I remember one clump of high, feathery grass which was a regular bandstand for the katydid musicians.

By nine o'clock, the activity of the night insects is in full swing. By midnight, many of the little creatures are tiring and, just before dawn, almost all of them have finished their night life and are tucking themselves in for a day of rest. To enjoy flashlight hunting does not mean that you have to keep late hours. Any time after dusk, you can set out on your trip of exploration.

As you train your circle of light on the grass, you

will see little black crickets hurrying past; gray daddy longlegs hobbling by with their seedlike bodies bobbing up and down; pale green cone-headed grasshoppers moving through the forest of grass blades. On a weed-top, your beam picks out a katydid, balancing itself like a tightrope walker while it fiddles out its endlessly repeated song. Busily investigating a golden sunflower, you see two small brown moths and on the leaves of several plants there are night beetles which have climbed up from the ground with the coming of dusk.

Oftentimes, in prowling among the trees of an old orchard on flashlight expeditions, I have seen hundreds of tiny gemlike spider webs, only an inch or two across, strung from twig to twig. Pale little spiders sit waiting for what the night's seining will bring them.

Whenever you come to a tree, run your beam slowly up and down along the trunk and branches. You may catch sight of the shy and beautiful snowy tree cricket, that melodious night singer whose music Hawthorne described as like "the sound of moonlight." These creatures are so pale green they look pure white in the rays of a flashlight. To produce their music, they raise their wings straight above their backs and vibrate them rapidly from side to side. Perhaps you will be fortunate enough to see the curious feast which the male offers the female when she comes in response to his melodious fiddling. Each time he raises his wings, he reveals little cups which are filled with a fatty substance highly relished by the female. While he is fiddling, she mounts his back and begins her strange banquet—accompanied with music.

You can learn much about the sleeping habits of day insects by hunting with a flashlight at night. As you swing your beam from plant to plant and from tree to tree, you see insect sleepers, oblivious to what is going on around them. I have found bumblebees, caught away from their nests, clinging to the underside of a leaf and hanging back downward, so sound asleep they made no move even when I "shouted in their ears" and tapped the twig to which the leaf was attached. Another time, I came on a great metallic-blue dragon-fly, gripping the stalk of a nicotiana plant, "bedded down" for the night. On other occasions I have encountered Carolina locusts hanging upright on grass stems so sound asleep that when I picked them off they hardly struggled.

The habit of bees in hanging back-down when resting outdoors for the night, led to a curious theory which was accepted by naturalists centuries ago in the days of the Roman writer, Pliny. He wrote that the insects choose this position to prevent dew from settling on their wings and making them too heavy for flight when the morning came!

Getting acquainted with the night singers, so you can recognize the insects that produce the different trills and burrs and fiddlings, is part of the fun of after-dark exploring. You will soon learn the katydid's call, and know that the pulsing, rhythmical "waa-

waa-waa," repeated hour after hour, is the music of the snowy tree cricket. Some night, you will hear a buzz suggesting the sound of a tiny bandsaw coming from a clump of weeds or grass. Stealing closer, you will throw your beam on the clump and then with a quick grab catch the insect you see moving on the stems. It will be a slender, leaf-green grasshopper with what appears to be a fool's cap on its head. The name of this green musician is the cone-headed grasshopper. If your flashlight picks out one of these coneheads in the act of fiddling, you will see it hanging head downward, breathing rapidly as it plays.

Other night singers often will elude you. But that is what adds to the sport. I remember hunting for two summers for a peculiar ticking sound that came tantalizingly from the tallest maple trees in the neighborhood. Twice I heard the sound from lower bushes but arrived after it had stopped and, although I waited like a tree rooted to the spot, the insect remained silent. The sound suggested a watch ticking loudly and going faster and faster until it suddenly stopped. Finally, just at dusk, I saw an angular-winged katydid in the very act of giving the call which had mystified me.

Learning the identity of insects that make the sounds you hear in the summer darkness, seeing what is going on in Insectland during nocturnal hours, and learning how the day insects spend their nights, are attractions that make hunting with a flashlight so fascinating.

Chapter XXIV

INSECT MUSICIANS

WHEN Raymond L. Ditmars, the famous curator of animals and reptiles at the Bronx Zoo in New York City, was a boy, he tried to assemble a katydid chorus. He collected a large number of the six-legged musicians, he once told me, and put them in cages. Selecting the ones that fiddled in different "keys" he tried to induce them all to play in unison.

You can have similar fun by going out with a flashlight after dark and collecting such celebrated insect fiddlers as the cone-head grasshopper, the black cricket, the katydid and the pale-green snowy tree cricket—the sweetest singer of all. As evening comes on, these musicians will begin to give their instrumental solos. Oftentimes, if you make a move or turn on a light in the room where the cages are kept, the music ceases instantly. In the Orient, where crickets are often kept as pets, the insects sometimes take the place of watchdogs. If an intruder enters the house, all the crickets stop chirping and the sudden silence awakens the owner!

Almost all members of the insect orchestra, except the loud-drumming cicada, belong to the Orthoptera

(Or-thop'-tera) order. In these insects, the second pair of wings fold like a fan and fit under the first pair. Among the orthoptera are the grasshoppers, the crickets and the katydids. In almost every case, the front wing-covers provide the "fiddle and the bow" with which the little musician scrapes out his tunes. "His" is right. Almost all six-legged music-makers are males, the females having wings without the fiddles.

You can examine the wings of dead musical insects and, after they are removed, try to produce sounds by scraping them together. Near the base of their wings, katydids and crickets, the two most famous members of the six-legged orchestra, have roughened files and thin stiff ridges or scrapers. By moving their wings, they grate the file along the scraper and produce their instrumental solos. Katydids usually fold their wings with the left overlapping the right, thus bringing the ridge below the file, while crickets nearly always fold the right wing over the left one, exactly the reverse of the katydids, and play with the ridge above the file.

When the katydid says "she-did," it has rasped its wings together twice. When it says "Ka-ty-did," it has rasped them together three times. A scientist once calculated that, in the course of a summer season, a katydid rasps its file and ridge together as many as 50,-000,000 times! On warm nights, one of these familiar insects will repeat "katy-did, katy-did, katy-did" as many as sixty times a minute.

Besides the true katydid, with oval wings, there are several other kinds, each with a ticking or rasping sound of its own. Oftenest, these leaf-green creatures are found among the foliage of trees and bushes. On rare occasions, they are bright pink instead of green. In the autumn, females cement their eggs in a border around leaves and onto twigs. The eggs are flat, oval and slate gray.

Grasshopper musicians are of two kinds: the long-horns and the short-horns. The former have antennae that are long and slender—often far longer than the body of the insects. They are the true grasshoppers. The short-horned insects, with antennae much shorter than their bodies, are locusts.

Commonest of these latter music-makers are the Carolina locusts, those gray-brown mottled creatures that show their brilliant under-wings when they hover in the air or sail away over the weeds of an open field. The clattering sound they produce—like the clicking of castanets—is made by the wings themselves rattling as they move. Some locusts give off a crackling noise which carries as far as a quarter of a mile.

One brown little fellow, less than an inch long, produces its "music" in a different way. It scrapes its roughened thighs against sharp-edged veins on its wings to bring forth a dry little song something like "tsikk-tsikk-tsikk." As a whole, the locusts are more famous for their vast numbers during plagues and for the "tobacco juice" saliva they eject when you hold them, than they are as music-makers.

It is the long-horned grasshoppers that provide some

of the best fiddling in the night concert. Their music is always produced by rubbing wing against wing. If you listen on sultry summer nights, you will hear a variety of sounds made by these fiddlers. One is a long-drawn "Zeeeeeeee!" It is metallic and ear-piercing. This is the song of the cone-headed grasshopper.

The first of the insect musicians to tune up its fiddle each year is the common black cricket. Turn over an old board or a flat stone, late in August, and you will find scores of these lively insects. The strong, clear "chirp" of the cricket is known throughout the world. The house cricket, a relative of the black field insect, lives in dwellings all winter and gives its little serenades each evening.

Another relative is the humble mole cricket. It spends its life digging just below the surface with flattened front feet, making tunnels in damp soil and eating roots and underground worms. At night, you can hear its steady "churr-churr-churr" coming from marshy fields or streambanks. It usually sits in the mouth of its tunnel and sings when darkness comes. Occasionally, it flies abroad and is attracted to electric lights. This cricket is the largest of the family. Its hard, shell-like body has given it the nickname of "earth crab."

Before she lays her eggs, the female mole cricket hollows out a nest shaped like half an egg cut lengthwise. Around it, she tunnels a network of connecting passageways in which she hides, guarding the eggs from enemy beetles and also from the father of her offspring, for the male mole cricket is a cannibal that eats his own children if he has a chance!

The handsomest of the crickets and, at the same time, the most beautiful instrumentalist of the whole night orchestra, is the snowy tree cricket. It is the only one of the six-legged fiddlers that appears to feel it is part of a group of players. When you hear the common snowy tree crickets begin their melodious "waa-waa-waa" or "treat-treat-treat," when evening comes, you will notice that those in the same bush or tree will start out as individual players, then they will all join together and keep the same time as though led by a conductor waving a baton.

When playing, the insects move their wings so fast, they appear merely as a blur when seen in a flashlight beam. One listener counted the number of successive trills made by a tree cricket. He found that the insect repeated its musical note 2640 times before it paused. The number of beats a minute varies with the heat of the night. Thus, the snowy tree cricket has been called "the Temperature Cricket." If you count the number of pulsations a minute in its music and divide by four and then add forty, you will have the temperature in Fahrenheit degrees.

In conclusion, here is a list of some of the common insect solos together with the names of the musicians producing them. Of course, these sounds cannot be reproduced exactly in words, but the following approximations will give you a clue to unknown singers. The best way to solve a mystery in regard to an unknown six-legged singer is to stalk it with a flashlight. When you capture the insect you think is making the sound, bring it home and place it in a cage. It is likely that the next evening, when it has become accustomed to its surroundings, it will perform for you. A few of the insects listed below make more than one sound. The one you are most likely to hear is given.

"Waa—Waa—Waa—"	(Mellow and rhythmical)	Snowy Tree Cricket
"Zip! Zip! Zeeeeee!"	(Shrill)	Meadow Grass-hopper
"Chirp! Chirp!"	(Clear and ringing)	Black Cricket
"Katy-Did! Katy-Didn't!"	(Repeated)	The True Katydid
"Tzeet! Tzeet! Tzeet!"	(Repeated rapidly)	Angular-Winged Katydid
"Zeeeeeeeeee!"	(High-pitched, ear-piercing buzz)	Cone-headed Grasshopper
"Churr!—Churr—Churr—"	(Repeated steadily)	Mole Cricket

Chapter XXV

KEEPING AN INSECT ZOO

ONE of the best ways of becoming acquainted with many six-legged creatures is to keep them in an insect zoo. A number, including most of the fiddlers in the night orchestra, thrive in captivity. Compared with rabbits and other animal pets, insects eat little and occupy only a small space. Several of them will live indoors far into the autumn and winter.

If you are located in a part of the country where the praying mantis is found, start your zoo with it. It does not even require a cage. Place it on a house plant or curtain and it will cling, oftentimes in one place, for hours. In a wild state, the mantis eats nothing but living prey. Indoors, I have found I could feed my captives on bits of meat, such as corned beef or hamburg steak, offered at the end of a toothpick or a pair of tweezers. The insect grasps its food in its forelegs and devours it like a boy eating an ear of corn.

If you provide a cage for your praying mantises, you can place grasshoppers, crickets and other living insects inside. In the course of time, they will be captured and eaten by the carnivorous mantises. Like the black cricket, the mantis is cannibalistic. So don't put big and small mantises in the same cage. When I did that once, I found, at the end of an hour, a little pile of wings and legs, all that remained of a medium-sized inmate of the cage. Besides its diet of meat, give a captive mantis water to drink each day. Sprinkle the wire of the cage so it is covered with "dew" morning and night and the mantis will get sufficient moisture.

In the fall, collect the female mantises and place them on twigs stuck in jars of water or in wet sand so they will keep fresh. If you have half a dozen or so of the females, you are likely to see one or more make the curious froth ball which solidifies and protects the eggs of the insect over the winter. The process takes from one to three hours and is a sight you will never forget. Once, one of my captive mantises made her egg case on a windowsill just above a radiator. The heat hastened the hatching so the young insects appeared exactly on the first day of winter, December 21st.

Another curious insect that eats nothing but living prey when it is in its wild state is the ant-lion, or doodlebug. Also, like the mantis, it can be kept without any special cage. All that is needed is a box or pan of fine sand. The ant-lions will dig tiny round depressions in the sand, tossing the material out with explosive jerks of their heads. Then, hidden at the bottom, they wait for some ant to slide down into the pit they have dug. With long pincer-jaws, they grab the luckless insect and begin at once to devour it. By placing a few ants in the dirt-box, you can feed your doodlebug captives. Almost any sandy stretch will provide you with ant-lions for your zoo. With a scoop of your hand, dig under one of their depressions and you will bring the doodlebug to the surface. Once, I saw one of these gray, flat, little creatures almost fall prey to another of its kind. In sidling over the sand in search of a place to dig its pit, it fell into the depression of another ant-lion which promptly tried to eat it.

For your katydids, walking sticks, grasshoppers and other large insects, you can construct a satisfactory cage by tacking wire screen to a simple framework, about two feet wide, three feet long and two feet high. This will give you room for a number of insects that feed on leaves and not on each other. The top should be hinged or removable. Inside, you can have leafy twigs stuck in sand which is kept damp, or in jars containing water. Be sure to get the same kind of twigs as those on which you found the inmates of the cage. Katydids seem to favor the leaves of cherry, oak, maple and apple trees. But they can be kept happy on a diet of lettuce and fruit. Grasshoppers like fresh grass, clover and almost any kind of fruit. Most grasshoppers are particularly fond of fresh corn silk. Walking sticks, like katydids, should be given the leaves of the trees or bushes on which they are found. Leaves and more leaves form their diet.

Crickets are easy to keep if a few simple rules are observed. The big black cricket you catch in the fields will eat both meat and vegetables. It is always well to add a bit of meat or bone meal from time to time to the regular rations of lettuce, fruit, moistened bread, and, what they enjoy especially, bits of melon. If you do not feed your crickets meat occasionally, they will take matters into their own hands and begin devouring each other.

A simple cricket cage which will enable you to see everything that takes place inside can be made by combining a lantern chimney and a flowerpot as is shown in Fig. 24. Fill the pot with dirt and place a

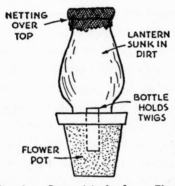

Fig. 24.—Rearing Cage Made from Flower Pot and Lantern Chimney.

twig in the jar of water which is embedded in the center. Then put the lantern globe in place, pushing it down into the dirt. Place your captives inside and cover the top of the chimney with a bit of mosquito netting, held in place by means of a rubber band. The netting can be removed when food and water are given the crickets and the chimney can be pulled out of the dirt when twigs are changed.

Among the beetles, there are many which you can

keep in your zoo. Some will thrive in a lantern-chimney cage such as has been described. An even better home for captive beetles consists of a flat block of plaster of Paris containing two hollowed-out depressions, a large one and a small one. The small one is filled with water which gradually seeps through to the large one in which the beetles live, thus keeping it in a moist condition. A pane of glass placed over the top of the plaster block will keep the beetles from escaping and will permit you to see all that takes place inside.

One of the most interesting corners of your insect zoo probably will be made up not of insects but of "worms." The caterpillars of various moths and butterflies are easy to keep and they provide an exciting show in several acts. You will see them grow and shed their skins; you will see them make their amazing change into cocoons and chrysalises; and finally, you will see them appear transformed into beautiful creatures of the air.

The larva should get sunlight and plenty of fresh leaves of its favorite tree or plant. Note where you find each caterpillar and supply it with the same sort of leaves. In looking for butterfly caterpillars, the following tips may help you. Look for Tiger Swallowtail caterpillars on wild cherry; Cabbage butterfly caterpillars on cabbage; Black Swallowtail caterpillars on carrots, parsley and wild ginger; Thistle butterfly caterpillars on burdock; Monarch caterpillars on milkweed; Viceroy caterpillars on poplar and willow; Buckeye caterpillars on plantain and snapdragon; Clouded

Sulphur caterpillars on clover; Red Admiral caterpillars on hops and nettles; and the little American Copper caterpillars on sorrel.

Among the moth larvae, some of the favored foods are: Luna: walnut, hickory, sweet gum and persimmon. Cecropia: willow, maple, lilac. Polyphemus: oak and birch. Ailanthus: wild cherry, lilac, ailanthus, linden. Promethea: wild cherry. Darling Underwing: willow, poplar.

You can use lantern-globe cages for your caterpillars or you can make a larger cage by pasting mosquito netting across the top of a shoe box. Or you can produce a cheap "community wormery" by tacking wire screen over a soapbox. Without any indoor cage at all, you can raise caterpillars on the trees where they are naturally found by doing what is known as "sleeving" a branch. Slip a cylinder of mosquito netting over the branch and tie it tight at both ends. Within this net, the caterpillar lives a natural life with abundant fresh food. If the larva is one that pupates in the ground, you will have to extend the sleeve to a flowerpot filled with earth in which the larva can make its chrysalis. Incidentally, it is a good idea to have some pots or boxes of dirt in your caterpillar cages. Some of the captives may be larvae that descend into the ground for their change into chrysalises, instead of making their cocoons on twigs or forming the chrysalises on the tree or plant on which they feed.

When you place twigs in jars of water within cages for caterpillars to feed on, be sure to stuff cotton batting or rags around the top of the container holding the water. Otherwise, the caterpillars may crawl down and get drowned. Instead of water or wet sand, you can sometimes use potatoes to keep twigs fresh for a considerable time. Stick the end of the twig into the potato. It provides moisture and a base for the twig at the same time. Because larvae use only very small amounts of air, you can sometimes keep their food fresh by enclosing both leaves and larva in a Mason jar with the lid tightly screwed in place. This prevents evaporation and so keeps the leaves juicy and green.

Most caterpillars are like kittens. They do not thrive if handled too much. Also, many have sharp spines which discourage people from handling them. The best way of transferring a caterpillar, both for you and the larva, is to carry it on a twig or by means of an old discarded tablespoon. When several of your "worms" have changed into chrysalises, it is a good idea to remove the remaining caterpillars to another cage. Sometimes, when food runs low, caterpillars will begin gnawing on the chrysalises if they are left in the same place.

If you keep a "logbook" of the occurrences in your insect zoo, it will increase your sport greatly. Put down the date and the hour when you see, for example, eggs being laid, when they hatch out, when the molting, pupation and emergence of the adult occur. The more notes you have, the more interesting things you will learn. Just as it has been discovered that butterflies emerge frequently before a thunderstorm; that mantis egg cases hatch out most often between eight and nine in the morning; that the speed of ants is governed by the heat of the day, so you may discover interesting facts by watching the inmates of your insect zoo and keeping a "log" of the things you see.

Chapter XXVI

LIFE HISTORIES

IMAGINE the thrill of having a beautiful butterfly named after you!

A friend of mine, Sidney A. Hessel, experienced that honor in 1950. The previous spring, he and two companions, George W. Rawson and J. Benjamin Ziegler, had been collecting in the pine barrens of southern New Jersey. This lonely stretch of cedar bogs and pitch-pine scrub lies only fifty miles south of New York City and only twenty miles east of Philadelphia. For generations, big-city butterfly collectors have been combing the area. Yet all the while the new hairstreak discovered by these three amateurs had been living unnoticed amid the white cedars of isolated bogs. The wings of this beautiful midget are brownish-black above and iridescent green with markings of brown and white below. Named *Mitoura hesseli*, or Hessel's Hairstreak, it is the first new butterfly added to the lists of science from the northeastern United States in forty years.

Such an achievement is the dream of every butterfly collector. But in this case the three discoverers did not rest on their honors. They haunted the cedar bogs.

They found the green eggs and the green-and-white caterpillars of the butterfly. They noted what the larva ate, kept records of the different stages in its development, brought larvae home, watched the formation of the pupa and recorded the length of time before the winged adult appeared. Thus they became acquainted with the whole life-cycle of the insect they had discovered. When, in June 1950, they published the results of their watching in the *Journal of the New York Entomological Society*, they added a new chapter to the story of American butterflies.

Surprisingly few insects have been studied in this way. In the case of the majority of species, even the main events in their lives are still unrecorded. There are literally thousands of small moths whose caterpillars and food-plants are unknown. The discoverers of new insects too often have lost interest after the christening party. They have been content to name the creature and then forget about it. Insects have to be named; that is the starting point. But as Benjamin Franklin observed, a century and a half ago, what is the use of naming things if we know not the things we name?

In the last chapter, I told of the fun of having an insect zoo. You can increase that fun by keeping records of the life histories of the various winged and creeping creatures in your cages. When you return from the fields with an unknown larva, feed it on the plant on which you found it, watch it mature and finally transform into an adult insect, you solve a riddle and have an adventure at the same time. It is like reading a detective story. You don't know how it turns out until the end. You don't know what your insect is until you come to the last chapter of its life.

Oftentimes you will discover insect eggs on the leaves of various plants. Bring them in and you start at the very beginning of the life-cycle of the insects that hatch from them. Your logbook of the progress of these creatures may possibly record the successive steps in the life of some insect whose history has previously been unknown. Thus your hobby can combine fun and real adventure.

Most professional entomologists are engaged in problems of identification or problems of controlling insect pests. They are in museum or government employ. Hence the amateur, with his spare-time hobby of insect exploring, has a wide-open field in the study of life histories and habits. It was an amateur, Frank Morton Jones, a Delaware businessman, who discovered facts about the familiar bagworm that scientists had never known before. He found how the caterpillar anchors its bag with bands of silk when it wants to feed and he solved the riddle of how the winged male mates with the wingless female. Another amateur, Phil Rau, the owner of a store in Missouri, became engrossed in watching digger wasps in a vacant lot one morning as he was on his way to work. All the rest of his life, he was a student of these remarkable insects. Some of his observations, recorded in *Wasp Studies Afield*, have been referred to in a previous chapter. His patient outdoor observations contributed greatly to our knowledge of these insects.

Lord Avebury, the English student of the ants, carried on his experiments at odd moments in a busy political life. He was a pioneer in stressing the importance of knowing the lives and habits of specimens collected. "To place stuffed birds and beasts in glass cases, to arrange insects in cabinets and dried plants in drawers," he wrote, "is merely the drudgery and preliminary of study. To watch their habits, to understand their relations to one another, to study their instincts and intelligence, to ascertain their adaptations and their relations to the forces of nature, to realize what the world appears to them, these constitute the true interest of natural history." This viewpoint, the study of the living creature in relation to its surroundings, is one that is being increasingly stressed by science. Even if you collect every insect in your region, you still have exciting possibilities for adventure exploring unknown paths in connection with the lives of the creatures you have collected.

A good starting point for research is the food habits of different insects. Some insects, such as the cockroach, will eat almost anything. Others are specialists. Like men who want nothing but oyster stew or ham and eggs, they confine themselves to a single dish. They dine, for example, on the leaves of only one group of plants; in some cases, on those of only a single species of plant. Surrounded by quantities of luscious leaves of other kinds, they will starve to death rather than take a bite. So in bringing your larvae in from the fields, be sure you also bring the plants on which you find them feeding.

One of the most remarkable instances of specialized feeding that I know was related to me, not long ago, by Rowland R. McElvare, a specialist in the Heliothid moths. Many of these moths feed on wild asters. South of the Salton Sea, in southern California, a deep and narrow canyon cuts through a mountain near the Mexican border. Known as Split Mountain Canyon, it is several miles long and, in some places, hardly more than a hundred feet wide. Here, a few years ago, a botanist discovered a new species of aster. When news of the find reached Riverside, California, the thought occurred to an entomologist there:

"Wouldn't it be interesting if this new species of aster proved to be the food-plant of a new species of Heliothid moth?"

The following spring, an expedition to the remote canyon was arranged. On the bushy clumps of the aster, the entomologist captured a number of small Heliothids. He found them there and only there. Close examination showed they were unlike any previously collected. They were unknown to science—a new species of moth on a new species of aster.

At the opposite extreme from this discovery in a remote canyon was George P. Engelhardt's discovery in his own backyard. In 1946, the Smithsonian Institution, in Washington, D. C., published his monograph on the clear-wing moths of North America.

From the time it was first described in 1881 until 1936, one clear-wing was rarely captured. For many years, in an attempt to work out its life-history, Engel-hardt sought the larva of this rare species. Once he heard a rumor that the moth was abundant in an area in western Canada. He made a collecting trip of thou-sands of miles without finding it. Then, in 1936, as he was clearing out some damaged vines of Virginia creeper in his yard at Hartsdale, New York, he dis-covered borers in the stems. Taking them indoors he raised them to maturity. The moths that resulted were the rarely captured insects. The borers in the vines just outside his door were the long-sought larvae. They provided him with the first and only food-plant and rearing record for the species and the first record of the occurrence of the insect in the state of New York —and they enabled him to complete the life story of the clear-wing.

If you try your hand at raising insects with special-ized tastes in food, it is a good idea to be sure the supply of that food is ample before you begin. One summer when Roger Tory Peterson was a boy in Jamestown, N. Y., he collected several hundred cater-pillars of the pipevine swallowtail. As the supply of pipevine leaves diminished in the autumn, he ranged farther and farther from home in his search for food for his caterpillars. He spent more and more hours foraging for the only fodder the larvae would eat. But in the end he brought every caterpillar through and saw it safely changed into a pupa.

While butterfly and moth larvae are relatively
simple to raise, other kinds of insects can also be
watched throughout the successive stages of their development. You can keep ant-lions in boxes of sand.
You can keep aphis-lions on potted plants infested with
plant lice. You can keep dragonfly nymphs and other
water insects in small aquariums. You can raise katydids and crickets. And, in doing so, you will learn
much about the food preferences of each, about its
abilities and its appearance at different periods of its
life.

One of the great names in the history of butterfly-
study in the United States is William Henry Edwards.
His monumental *Butterflies of North America* appeared in three volumes between the years 1868 and
1897. Although this amateur lived in an isolated West
Virginia community, at first accessible only by stage-
coach, he had butterfly eggs shipped to him from
California, Texas, Arizona and Florida. By raising the
insects, he was able to work out their life histories and
record in drawings the different forms of the developing larvae.

Beginning with the egg usually eliminates the pos-
sibility of getting a parasite instead of the insect you
desire. Caterpillars and pupae are more likely to be
infested. Once as I started to photograph the transformation of a monarch larva that had attached itself
to the underside of a milkweed leaf, the caterpillar
went suddenly limp. Parasites within had killed it.
Then the white grubs of a parasitic fly appeared

through the skin of the caterpillar, slid down to a leaf below, wriggled off to the soil underneath and there burrowed out of sight to pupate beneath the surface. In a sequence of pictures, which appear in one of my nature books, *Days Without Time*, I was able to record the larva, the pupa and the adult of this curious parasite.

If you have a camera that will photograph small objects, you can obtain pictures of the various stages of development in the insects you raise. If not, drawings, even crude ones, will be immensely helpful in keeping a detailed record of your observations. In making notes, it is better to put down too much rather than too little. Don't trust to your memory. Be sure you see exactly what happens. If possible, try to see everything more than once. And whenever you are in doubt, put a query beside your notation. By observing these rules, you will add to the value as well as the fun of recording life histories.

Chapter XXVII

WINTER WORK

WHEN the insect musicians cease fiddling and butterflies are no longer on the wing, when the brilliant
leaves of autumn have fallen to the ground and winter
cold is on its way, your insect exploring seems to have
come to an end. However, you can find fun in winter
as well as in summer among the insects. Only, it is a
different kind of fun.

During the months of cold, you have a chance to
examine your specimens closely, to see things you
missed, to identify exactly insects you failed to recognize before. You can put your collection in order,
arranging the specimens to best advantage and getting
the labels neatly written and in place.

While the winds howl outside, you can add to the
interest of your exhibits by dramatizing unusual facts
about insects. For example, you can put "look-alikes"
together—Monarch butterflies and their mimics the
Viceroys, bumblebees and flies that resemble them,
and so on. You can assemble a "Bug Band," placing the
different music-makers, the katydids, cicadas, grasshoppers, and crickets, together. You can recruit an Insect Army, including the insects that do different

things required of soldiers in real warfare. This would include camouflage artists such as the Darling Underwing moth; trench-diggers like the mole cricket and various bettles; "liquid fire" throwers, like the wood ants that eject a burning acid; gas-attack experts like the bombardier beetles; stinging insects like the wasps and bees; and an air corps consisting of winged insects like dragonflies and robber flies. Explanatory labels under the different "soldiers" in this six-legged army would bring out the curious abilities of each.

Another idea for an unusual mounted display is to assemble an "Insect Machine Shop," bringing together all the different insects that use tools. Mole crickets with their shovel forepaws, Ichneumon flies with their drill-like ovipositors for boring through wood, hornets and paper-making wasps with their pincer mandibles for chewing up woodpulp, digger wasps that use pebbles for hammers, leaf-cutting bees that have "scissors" for snipping off pieces of leaves, and termites that grind wood into sawdust.

A variation of this idea is a "Bug Labor Union," including the insects that do different kinds of work—carpenters, diggers, paper-makers, undertakers, tailors, candy-makers, hunters, fishers, trappers and masons. Again you can collect a "Parasite Zoo," placing parasites and their victims together.

Of course, such displays will be separate from your regular collections. They will provide fun for winter evenings and they will be attractive to friends who are not essentially interested in insects.

Besides going over your specimens in the winter-time you can go over your equipment and get it in shape for the coming summer season. You can make new nets and seines and gather together miscellaneous bottles and boxes for your next expeditions into the jungle of weeds and bushes where the insects live. You can construct more specimen boxes and can fold little bundles of paper triangles for future use. You can list the kinds of insects you need to fill in gaps in your collection. And, most of all, you can read more books on insects that will give you interesting facts about the lives of the little creatures you will meet. Reading about insects in the winter is a kind of "fun insurance," guaranteeing greater pleasure in your exploring the following season. Just as the fun of a game begins when you know the rules by heart, so the fun of insect exploring begins when you can recognize at sight the fascinating things that are taking place around your feet.

But all winter work is not done indoors. You can go on hunting trips even when the trees are bare and snow is on the ground. You can make a collection of the different kinds of galls, those curious bulges and strangely shaped bumps on twigs and the stems of weeds. Each has its story to tell. Each was formed when a small, winged insect laid its eggs in the plant tissues. These "living houses" within which the young insects developed are, of course, dead in winter. But they retain their forms and you can cut the stems and twigs and bring home a collection of the different kinds of galls.

Then, there are digging operations which you can carry on before the ground freezes hard. The first frosts kill off most of the insects. In the fall, the hornets and wasps and bumblebees, whose fiery stings have kept you at bay all summer, have died. You can dig carefully underground at spots where you have seen bumblebees and wasps entering nests in the earth. You can examine the cells and honeypot of the bumblebee, and the paper "combs" of the wasp. Also, you can cut open the big egg-shaped paper nests of the hornets and see what lies beneath the outer shell. You will find only a few unborn insects in the cells. All the other inmates of the great nest will be gone —killed while afield by the cold.

Before the ground becomes hard, you also can go on pupa-hunting expeditions. Many of the moth caterpillars change into chrysalises in the ground where they remain until spring. With a trowel, dig around the base of trees, particularly trees that are isolated in a meadow or are on the edge of a wood. Usually, you will find the best hunting on the north side. The caterpillars seem to know that on that side there will be less danger of excessive heat and drought during the latter part of summer when they are beginning their underground life. You can collect pupae during thaws in winter, as well as in fall. But early hunting is usually best. Mice and other pests destroy many of the chrysalises as the winter advances.

A few insects hibernate as adults. You can add these to your collection, making a special "Winter Insect" division. Ladybird beetles can be found under straw-stacks; carpenter ants can be located in the heart of old logs; water striders will be found hibernating in the trash around the edges of ponds and streams; bee-tles of various kinds are under loose bark, and the over-wintering mourning cloak butterflies sometimes can be located in hollow trees or can be caught as they flit about open glades on sunny days in February and March.

Then, there is the winter sport of cocoon hunting. You can collect the cocoons of large silk moths, such as the Polyphemus, Cecropia, Luna, Io and Promethea. When all the leaves have fallen from the trees and bushes, these yellow-brown envelopes holding the pupae can be seen easily. Cut the twig to which the cocoon is attached whenever possible. This will give the hatching moth a chance to support itself while its wings harden. During the winter, keep the cocoons in an attic or some building where they will not get too warm. Otherwise the moths will hatch out before spring. Sprinkle the cocoons with water once a week to prevent excessive dryness. Those not attached to twigs can be placed on dampened sphagnum moss where they will keep in good condition with no other attention than an occasional wetting of the moss.

From the last of March until June, a house with cocoons in it is an exciting place. The moths hatch out, sometimes during the night, sometimes during the day.

The first sign of the birth of some of these beautifully marked creatures is the dampening of one end of the cocoon. The insects eject an acid fluid from their mouths as they break from the pupa shell. This fluid softens and dissolves the silk of the cocoon, thus enabling the creatures to push their way through to freedom. The first appearance of the moth; its frantic search for a support where it can climb and hang while gravity pulls down its wings as they unfold and harden; the gradual drying of the furry body and fernlike antennae, and finally the flight of the great insect—all provide a thrilling show for the boy who has collected the cocoons.

And, when these gorgeous moths begin to appear, if you are an explorer among six-legged creatures, you have the added thrill of knowing that they are ushering in the beginning of another summer, another season of exciting excursions into the strange and absorbing world of the insects.

Bibliography

If you are interested in finding out more about the insect world and its curious inhabitants, the following list of books will aid you. A number of these volumes can be found on the shelves of any city library.

THE INSECT WORLD

A Lot of Insects, by Frank E. Lutz, Putnam, New York.

American Boy's Book of Bugs, Butterflies and Beetles, by Dan Beard, Lippincott, Philadelphia.

An Introduction to Entomology, by J. H. Comstock, Comstock Pub. Co., Ithaca, N. Y.

Ancient Artizans, by Stuart W. Frost, Van Press, Boston.

Everyday Doings of Insects, by Evelyn Cheesman McBride, New York.

Fabre's Book of Insects, by J. H. Fabre, Dodd, Mead, New York.

Grassroot Jungles, by Edwin Way Teale, Dodd, Mead, New York.

Handbook of Nature Study, by A. B. Comstock, Comstock, Ithaca, New York.

Insect Adventures, by J. H. Fabre, Dodd, Mead, New York.

Insect Invaders, by Anthony Standen, Houghton, Mifflin, Boston.

Insect Life, by Edwin Way Teale, Boy Scouts of America, New York.

Insect Life, by J. H. Comstock, Comstock, Ithaca, N. Y.

Insect Ways, by Clarence M. Weed, Appleton-Century, New York.

Marvels of Insect Life, by Edward Step, McBride, New York.

Near Horizons, The Story of an Insect Garden, by Edwin Way Teale, Dodd, Mead.

Our Insect Friends and Foes, by William Atherton DuPuy, Winston, Philadelphia.

Our Insect Friends and Foes and Spiders, by W. J. Showalter, National Geographic, Washington, D. C.

The Clever Little People With Six Legs, by Hallam Hawksworth, Scribners, New York.

The Insect World of J. Henri Fabre, edited by Edwin Way Teale, Dodd, Mead, New York.

The Outline of Science, by J. Arthur Thomson, Putnam, New York.

The World of Insects, by Gayle Pickwell and Carl C. Duncan, McGraw-Hill, New York.

COLLECTING INSECTS

Directions for Collecting and Preserving Insects, by Alexander B. Klotz, Ward's Natural Science Establishment, Rochester, N. Y.

Fieldbook of Insects, by Frank E. Lutz, Putnam, New York.

How to Collect and Preserve Insects, by Frank E. Lutz, American Museum of Natural History, New York.

How to Know the Insects, by H. E. Jaques, Wm. C. Brown & Co., Dubuque, Iowa.

Insects, by Herbert S. Zim and Clarence Cottam, Simon and Schuster, New York.

Insects, by Frank Balfour-Browne, Holt, New York.

Introducing the Insects, by F. A. Urquhart, Holt, New York.

Picture Book of Insects, by Albro T. Gaul, Lothrop, New York.

The Insect Guide, by Ralph B. Swain, Doubleday, New York.

BUTTERFLIES AND MOTHS

A Field Guide to the Butterflies, by Alexander B. Klots, Houghton, Mifflin, Boston.

Among the Moths and Butterflies, by Julia P. Ballard, Putnam, New York.

Butterfly and Moth Book, by Ellen Robertson-Miller, Scribners, New York.
How to Know Butterflies, by A. B. Comstock, Comstock, Ithaca, N. Y.
Life of the Butterfly, by Friedrich Schnack, Houghton, Mifflin, Boston.
The Butterfly Book, by W. J. Holland, Doubleday, New York.
The Moth Book, by W. J. Holland, Doubleday, New York.
The Tale of the Promethea Moth, by Henry B. Kane, Knopf, New York.

BEETLES

American Boy's Book of Bugs, Butterflies and Beetles, by Dan Beard, Lippincott, Philadelphia.
Fieldbook of Insects, by Frank E. Lutz, Putnam, New York.
Handbook of Nature Study, by A. B. Comstock, Comstock, Ithaca, N. Y.
More Beetles, by J. H. Fabre, Dodd, Mead, New York.
The Glowworm and Other Beetles, by J. H. Fabre, Dodd, Mead, New York.
The Sacred Beetle and Others, by J. H. Fabre, Dodd, Mead, New York.

WASPS

American Social Insects, by Charles D. Michener and Mary H. Michener, Van Nostrand, New York.
Ants, Bees and Wasps, by John Lubbock, Dutton, New York.
Instinct and Intelligence, by R. W. G. Hingston, Macmillan, New York.
More Hunting Wasps, by J. H. Fabre, Dodd, Mead, New York.
The Hunting Wasps, by J. H. Fabre, Dodd, Mead, New York.
The Tale of the White-Faced Hornet, by Henry B. Kane, Knopf, New York.
The Witchery of Wasps, by E. G. Reinhard, Appleton-Century, New York.
Wasp Studies Afield, by Phil and Nellie Rau, Princeton University Press, Princeton, N. J.

Wasps and Their Ways, by W. M. Morley, Dodd, Mead, New York.

Wasps, Social and Solitary, by G. W. and E. G. Peckham, Houghton, Mifflin, Boston.

COLLECTING WITH A CAMERA

How to Make Good Pictures, Eastman Kodak Co., Rochester, N. Y.

Nature Photography Around the Year, by Percy A. Morris, Appleton-Century, New York.

The Photographic Magazines: *American Photography*, *Popular Photography*, etc.

DRAGONFLIES

A Handbook of the Dragonflies of North America, by James G. Needham and H. B. Heywood, Charles C. Thomas, Springfield, Illinois.

Fieldbook of Insects, by Frank E. Lutz, Putnam, New York.

Fieldbook of Ponds and Streams, by A. H. Morgan, Putnam, New York.

Handbook of Nature Study, by A. B. Comstock, Comstock, Ithaca, N. Y.

Natural History of Aquatic Insects, by L. C. Miall, Macmillan, New York.

The Biology of Dragonflies, by R. J. Tillyard, Cambridge University Press, London, England.

The Insect Book, by Leland O. Howard, Doubleday, New York.

ANTS

Ant Communities and How They Are Governed, by H. C. McCook, Harpers, New York.

Ants, by Julian Huxley, Cape and Smith, London and New York.

Ants, by William Morton Wheeler, Columbia University Press, New York.

Ants, Bees and Wasps, by John Lubbock, Dutton, New York.

Demons of the Dust, by William Morton Wheeler, Norton, New York.

Social Behavior in Insects, by A. D. Imms, Dial, New York.

The Astonishing Ant, by Julie C. Kenly, Appleton-Century, New York.

The Wonder World of the Ants, by Wilfrid S. Bronson, Harcourt, Brace, New York.

TERMITES

Our Enemy, the Termite, by Thomas E. Snyder, Comstock, Ithaca, N. Y.

Termite City, by Alfred E. Emerson and Eleanor Fish, Rand, McNally, Chicago.

Termites and Termite Control, by Charles E. Kofoid, University of California Press, Berkeley, Calif.

WALKING STICKS AND MANTISES

Book of Insects, by J. H. Fabre, Dodd, Mead, New York.

Fieldbook of Insects, by Frank E. Lutz, Putnam, New York.

Grassroot Jungles, by Edwin Way Teale, Dodd, Mead, New York.

Our Insect Friends and Foes, by William Atherton DuPuy, Winston, Philadelphia.

Praying Mantids of the United States, by Ashley B. Gurney, Smithsonian Institution, Washington, D. C.

The Grasshopper Book, by Wilfrid S. Bronson, Harcourt, Brace, New York.

WATER INSECTS

A Multitude of Living Things, by Lorus J. Milne and Margery J. Milne, Dodd, Mead, New York.

Fieldbook of Insects, by Frank E. Lutz, Putnam, New York.

Fieldbook of Ponds and Streams, by A. H. Morgan, Putnam, New York.

Insect Life, by J. C. Bradley and E. L. Palmer, Boy Scouts of America, New York.

Life of Inland Waters, by J. G. Needham and J. T. Lloyd, Comstock, Ithaca, N. Y.

BEES

Ants, Bees and Wasps, by John Lubbock, Dutton, New York.

Bees, Their Vision, Chemical Senses, and Language, by Karl Von Frisch, Cornell University Press, Ithaca, N. Y.

Bramblebees and Others, by J. H. Fabre, Dodd, Mead, New York.

Bumblebees and Their Ways, by O. E. Plath, Macmillan, New York.

Children of the Golden Queen, by Flora McIntyre, E. P. Dutton & Co., Inc., New York.

Cities of Wax, by Julie C. Kenly, Appleton-Century, New York.

The Bee People, by M. W. Morley, McClurg, Chicago.

The Hive and the Honeybee, by Roy A. Grout, Dadant & Sons, Hamilton, Illinois.

The Honey Makers, by M. W. Morley, McClurg, Chicago.

The Life of the Bee, by Maurice Maeterlinck, Dodd, Mead, New York.

HOW TO KEEP BEES

Beekeeping, by E. F. Phillips, Macmillan, New York.

How to Keep Bees, by A. B. Comstock, Comstock, Ithaca, N. Y.

Starting Right With Bees, by H. G. Rowe, A. I. Root Co., Medina, O.

The ABC and XYZ of Bee Culture, by E. R. Root, A. I. Root Co., Medina, O.

FLIES

American Boy's Book of Bugs, Butterflies and Beetles, by Dan Beard, Lippincott, Philadelphia.

Fieldbook of Insects, by Frank E. Lutz, Putnam, New York.

Handbook of Nature Study, by A. B. Comstock, Comstock, Ithaca, N. Y.

The Life of the Fly, by J. H. Fabre, Dodd, Mead, New York.

The Natural History of Mosquitoes, by Marston Bates, Macmillan, New York.

Bibliography

MUSICAL INSECTS

American Insects, by Vernon Kellogg, Holt, New York.

Fieldbook of Insects, by Frank E. Lutz, Putnam, New York.

Grasshopperland, by M. W. Morley, McClurg, Chicago.

The Insect Book, by Leland O. Howard, Doubleday, New York.

The Life of the Grasshopper, by J. H. Fabre, Dodd, Mead, New York.

END

Index